Talks Your *Dad*
Never Had with *You*

D1456488

Talks Your *Dad*
Never Had with *You*

Dr. Harold D. Davis

MOODY PUBLISHERS

CHICAGO

All Scripture quotations, unless otherwise indicated, are taken from *The New Century Version®*. Copyright © 1987, 1988, 1991 by Word Publishing, Nashville, TN 37214. Used by permission. All rights reserved.

Scripture quotations marked TLB are taken from *The Living Bible* copyright © 1971. Used by permission of Tyndale House Publishers, Inc., Wheaton, Illinois 60189. All rights reserved.

Scripture quotations marked NKJV are taken from the *New King James Version*. Copyright © 1982 by Thomas Nelson, Inc. Used by permission. All rights reserved.

Scripture quotations marked AMP are taken from *The Amplified Bible*. Copyright © 1965, 1987 by The Zondervan Corporation. *The Amplified New Testament* copyright © 1958, 1987 by The Lockman Foundation. Used by permission.

Editor: Kathryn Hall
Interior Design: Ragont Design
Cover Design: Trevell Southall, TS Design Studio (www.tsdesignstudio.net)
Cover Image: Getty Images

Library of Congress Cataloging-in-Publication Data

Davis, Harold D.
    Talks your dad never had with you / Harold D. Davis.
      p. cm.
    ISBN 978-0-8024-6251-0
    1. Teenage girls—Religious life. 2. Teenage girls—Conduct of life. 3. Fathers and daughters—Religious aspects—Christianity. I. Title.

BV4551.3.D37 2008
248.8'33—dc22

                                                                    2008003383

                        ISBN-10: 0-8024-6251-0
                        ISBN-13: 978-0-8024-6251-0

                    1 3 5 7 9 10 8 6 4 2

                Printed in the United States of America.

Contents

Part 5

Boys Will Be Boys

Part 6

Can Dad Love Me?

Part 7

God Is Your Father

Preface

THE RELATIONSHIP OF a father and daughter is very precious in the sight of a healthy father. Sadly, many father/daughter relationships are strained and stretched out of shape by the pressures of a contemporary society. The fact that many dads are absent or abusive is repeated in the media until one becomes sick of it.

To address these kinds of issues, a young lady needs to be aware of and benefit from the wisdom that comes from a loving father. Knowing how a healthy father thinks will help you understand your relationship with your own father and the men in your life. Such knowledge will also give you insight into the mind of a father who is fulfilling his role as a loving, caring, sensitive protector and provider for his children.

Wise parents use everyday events to teach their children about life. Everyday events can serve as object lessons and a stimulus to generate valuable conversations. In this book, Dad gives you his mind on a variety of issues as they arise in everyday life. My goal is to provide a healthy, fatherly perspective for young ladies to use as a reference as you make everyday decisions in your life.

I believe that in spite of the negative climate and the status of your current relationship with your father, God can bring healing and a healthy perspective to your understanding of what a relationship between a father and his daughter should be like.

I pray God's blessings upon you as you read the messages found on the following pages.

Introduction

To You, Daughter

THE FIRST THING that I would say to you is that you are intelligent, insightful, witty, and considerate— just like your mother. The second thing that you should be aware of is that you are my heart and you have my heart, so please be careful not to break it. Now that you are changing from a young girl to a woman, I want you to know that every day I pray that God will bless and keep you in the times ahead when you are faced with so many decisions and challenges. I want you to take your time and drink your milk shake, and I am going to tell you some of the things that are on my mind.

Love,

Daddy

Part 1

You Are Special

1—Daddy's Little Girl

Here's the Deal...

When you entered this world, I was the first man, other than our doctor, to touch you. I was amazed when you were wrapped in a blanket and given to me so that I could take you to the nursery. That was a big responsibility—to carry my newborn child to the nursery. Today you are a big girl, but I want you to know that I still have a strong sense of responsibility to protect you in every way and help you maintain two of the most important things about you—your integrity and your virginity. Let's talk.

FROM THE beginning of time dads have struggled with the idea that boys become sexually interested in their daughters as they grow up. Most dads who have been blessed with beautiful daughters cringe when they consider the thoughts that young men think about their prized possessions. You cannot understand this because it takes a father to know how another man thinks.

God made the role of fathers to provide a covering for their daughters. This makes the premature loss of virginity a major concern that a dad has for his daughter. I want you to know that my job as it relates to you is to provide for you and to protect you from anything or anybody who would hurt you. That includes defending your purity. As a protective dad I will not allow any boy to disrespect and abuse your emotions. I will do whatever is necessary to protect you—even if it means showing a boy that I'm willing to act a little crazy—if that's what it takes to get my point across to him.

With this in mind, I need you to help me stay out of trouble by using wisdom when interacting with the opposite sex. Because you are young and just learning about boys, you will need help in assessing their character. Promise me that when a boy shows an interest in you, you will always let him know that you have a dad who cares about you. In fact, tell the young man that you want him to meet your father. You may be surprised how this may help to keep his intentions in check.

The reason he needs to be aware of my presence is in case he is up to no good; knowing that I am watching over you will help deter him from disrespecting you. In some cases it won't help, but in most cases it will. Promise me that you will always remember this: before you spend any serious time with a young man, I want to meet him! Please don't think that doing this sounds lame and decide it's not worth putting your reputation with your friends on the line. God made you strong to stand up for what is right. He wants you to be a leader among your friends and let them know that they can also have the courage to choose right from wrong.

Most young girls don't think very clearly when they are interested in a young man, so they don't even realize that they need advice from someone who is older and has more experience. Please don't take this as a put-down; it's just the fact that young girls haven't had enough time to learn about the differences between boys and girls and what to watch out for. In fact, before they begin to explore their sexual urges, both girls and boys need to understand that love and infatuation are powerful emotions that need some serious boundaries.

Let me also say that many older girls don't think very clearly when they are interested in young men either; they need a second opinion too. It's not about how old you are when it comes to making good decisions on getting involved with boys. The truth is, people of all ages need help thinking through these issues. When you are just learning about boys, you need guidance in figuring out why boys think and behave the way they do. It will help you find out whether they are really sincere or if they just want to use you for a good time. That's where your dad's help becomes so important.

If a boy ever disrespects your desire to stay pure, drop him before you get hurt. Baby, I need you to talk to me about what is going on in your life. Throughout history, women have been protected by men. Human nature has not changed. Women still need to be protected, if not physically, then emotionally. If we communicate and you let me know what is going on, then I will be able to help you through your weak times. Everybody needs help through their weak times.

Growing up comes with its own set of challenges to face, such as the changes that take place in a girl's physical body, not to mention the social pressures that she also has to deal with. When she has to cope with these hard things without the guidance of a strong, positive father image to turn to for help, problems seem even more difficult to handle. Situations like these sometimes cause young girls to look for love and affection in the wrong places, which opens the door for them to get caught up in serious trouble. You may know of a girl who was abused by someone she trusted. That person really didn't care about her and only wanted to take advantage of her. She will most likely have big regrets that will stay with her for the rest of her life.

In fact, when girls grow into womanhood, the choices they made as young girls can still have an effect on them. It takes a lot of prayer and trust in God to overcome the mistakes that could have been avoided at a younger age. That is where the guidance and protection of a loving father can make a huge difference. Baby, I want you to know that I am here for you. I'm willing to help you in any way that I can as you work through this phase of your life.

You know, the Bible refers to the church as the bride of Christ because there is going to be a marriage one day between Jesus and His bride. This is the message that the apostle Paul taught in 2 Corinthians 11:2 because he wanted the church to live up to God's expectation and remain unpolluted so that Christ could marry a pure virgin. Paul compared the deep love that God desires us to show toward Him to a pure maiden who saves her love for one man only—her husband.

One major thing most dads are concerned about is their daughters being polluted by some slick dude who would like the opportunity to rob a girl of her virginity. It is a father's job to help his daughter avoid them. An earthly father wants the privilege of presenting his daughter as a bride untainted to her future husband just as the heavenly Father is planning to receive the church as the bride of Christ. You see, when we live our lives according to God's plan, God is pleased and we will reap the immense blessings God has as a reward for our obedience to Him. Our children and grandchildren will prosper also.

Besides the spiritual reasons for doing things God's way—which are the most important—there are practical reasons for living a pure life as well. With all of the diseases in the world today, taking a chance by having sex before marriage is just not worth it. In fact, because it is the right thing to do, young men should also be aware of the need for maintaining their purity and should be committed to wearing a ring of purity too. Your brother is going to get a ring and the same lecture, but my heart is with you in a different way than it is with him. I believe that females get hurt the most from premarital sex. They are hurt more emotionally, psychologically, and physically.

Making good choices will not only benefit you; it will also bless your mother and me. That is why the Bible tells you to "honor your father and mother." Ephesians 6:2 teaches that this is the first commandment that comes with a specific promise. When you give honor to your mother and me, you are opening the door for good things to happen in your life. That will bring us great joy and satisfaction, and God will reward you with a long and fruitful life.

Baby, if for no other reason, I want you to stay a virgin because this is God's desire for you, and I want you to live your life in a way that pleases Him. I have tried to do my part by living a godly life in front of you, and with God's help I have made good moral decisions. All I am asking is, on your wedding day you allow me the privilege to walk you down the aisle as my pure daughter. What do you say?

Think About It

1. Did this chapter help you
   understand how fathers feel about their daughters? Yes___ No___
   Why? Or why not?
   Explain _____

2. If your father is present in your life, do you have a good relationship
   with him? Yes___ No___ How has this affected your attitude about
   remaining pure until you are married?_____

   _____

3. Have you discussed the subject of purity with your father or a father
   figure? Yes___ No___ Why? Or why not?

   Explain _____

4. Do you think that TV programs present the same attitude about sex
   as a father who is concerned about his daughter does? Yes___
   No___ Why? Or why not?

   Explain _____

5. Would you introduce your boyfriend to your dad or father figure in
   the beginning of the relationship? Yes___ No___ Why? Or why not?

   Explain _____

6. Do you feel that introducing boys to your dad would end your social
   life? Yes___ No___ Why? Or why not?

   Explain _____

7. Do you talk to your father, mother, or some other responsible adult
   about what's going on in your personal life? Yes___ No___ Why?
   Or why not?

   Explain _____

8. Have you ever had to stop seeing a boy because he pressured you for
   sex? Yes___ No___ Why? Or why not?

   Explain _____

9. If you've already lost your virginity, did you know that God will forgive you and you can regain your purity?

2)—Our Special Agreement

Here's the Deal . . .

It dawns on me that you are growing up. I am aware that boys are really starting to notice you, and I also understand why they are noticing you. I realize that it is time for the two of us to discuss some important issues. So I plan an evening out at a fancy restaurant where we can talk. You are at the age when you do not talk a lot to Dad, so I have to pump you for conversation. Here is how the evening goes.

BABY, I WANT you to know that I enjoy being your father. You have brought me joy ever since you were born. I remember the first time I held you in my arms and thanked the Lord for you. I promised Him that with His help I would be a good father. I have also worked hard to keep the commitment I made to your mother when we got married, and the Lord has blessed me to be faithful. Now that you are moving into young adulthood, it is your turn to make a commitment to me, and with God's help, you will be faithful.

I take your left hand and point to the ring on your finger and ask you, "Where did you get that ring?" You respond that your mom gave it to you, and you also mention that it is gold plated. I reach in my pocket and present a ring to you and tell you that this ring is not gold plated, but solid gold. I continue to explain that I chose gold because gold is a precious metal that represents a precious promise. At this point, your face lights up and your mouth opens in surprise as you take the old ring off and put the new one on.

The ring that I just gave you is a promise ring that represents a covenant of purity. It stands for a special agreement between me and you. The agreement is that you will stay pure until your wedding day. Every time you look at this ring you should be reminded of that promise. On your wedding day, I will beam with pride as I walk you down the aisle. When the pastor says: "Who presents this woman to be married?" I will say: "Her mother and I do." Then you will take the ring off and give it to me and step over next to your soon-to-be husband. I will then keep this ring and cherish it until the day I die. Baby, I assure you that you can keep this promise, and I want you to always remember to pray, "I can do all things through Christ, because he gives me strength" (Philippians 4:13).

As a young lady, you should realize that the Bible has three positive classifications for women.

The virgin. This is a young lady who has never been sexually active, and her purity should be preserved until she marries. I feel that every man should protect and defend his unmarried daughter's purity. In ancient Israel, the virgins were guarded and protected from those who would exploit them.

Since a virgin is a girl who has not experienced sex, she is innocent. Her body has not been contaminated with the bacteria of another person, and she is considered pure. Her mind does not have an actual sexual memory to recall, so her thoughts about sex are not based on experience but on her imagination. Because she honors and respects God, her father, and herself, a girl who desires to remain pure will be careful not to allow any male to persuade her to have sexual relations before she is given in marriage. In fact, the Word of God goes so far as to say that until she is married her love should be for Christ alone

The married woman. This is a woman who is committed to her husband, and she is expected to be sexually active with him. The Bible commands it and encourages that married couples have sex on a regular basis.

The widow. This is a woman who may be young or old but whose husband has died. Widows are not to be sexually active unless they remarry. Young widows are encouraged to get married again if it is possible.

You, my dear, fall into the category of a virgin, one who has not become sexually active. I fall into the category of the father who is to protect you until the day when another man promises to take you as his wife and protect you always.

I hope you understand that maintaining your purity is a critical issue for a young lady. It may be a bit of a struggle sometimes, but it is well worth holding on to it. And you can overcome every obstacle that comes your way. Always remember that your promise ring is something for you to see and feel when you are confronted with temptations and trials.

God is pure and we are made in His image. First John 3:3 reminds us that since we are the children of God, we must live morally pure lives, just as our heavenly Father is pure. Just as I do, God wants you to remain pure until the day that your marriage commitment is fulfilled between you and your future husband.

If you keep your focus on Him, God will not fail you. There are a countless number of young ladies and young men who can attest to this truth. Don't believe the hype; it is possible to keep yourself pure until you are married in spite of the temptations that society offers to do otherwise.

I want you to promise me that you will stay pure until your wedding day. Is it a promise? (You look at me and say yes.) Because you've decided to keep this special promise, the Bible is very clear that this is a serious decision. That means God has a part in this agreement too. You can rest assured that He will keep His word, which says, "You must carefully obey everything in this agreement so that you will succeed in everything you do" (Deuteronomy 29:9).

Baby, if you ever need to talk, if you ever feel pressured, I want you to come and talk to me. Is that a deal? You respond: "Yes, Dad, it's a deal."

We continue to enjoy our evening reflecting occasionally on the commitment we just made. We conclude our evening of sharing good food and fun conversation.

Think About It

I. Have you made a covenant (or promise) with anyone about your purity? Yes____ No____ Why? Or why not?
Explain _____

2. If you haven't already, would you like to make that covenant? Yes____ No____ If yes, with whom would you like to make the covenant?
_____

3. How long should a young lady agree to wear a ring of purity?
_____

4. Do you feel that it is possible to remain pure until you are married? Yes____ No____ Why or why not?

Explain _____

5. Do you feel that it is fair for a parent to expect a daughter or son to stay pure until married? Yes____ No____

Explain your answer. _____

_____

6. Do you feel that you could keep a purity agreement if you made one? Yes____ No____ Why or why not?

Explain _____

7. Name the people in your life who would be excited to know that you have made a commitment to purity.

_____

8. Can you name anyone who would be disappointed by your decision to stay pure? For example, a young man who could be planning to use you for his pleasure.

_____

9. Are you committed to walking down the aisle as a virgin on your wedding day? Yes____ No____ Why or why not?

Explain _____

3)—It's All about Hugs

Here's the Deal . . .

You notice that some of the girls at school are always letting the boys hug them. In fact, it seems like they enjoy and need the hugging and touching they get from those boys. This is what your dad has to say about it.

BABY, EVER SINCE you were a little girl I have hugged you. I can remember when I used to squeeze you and rub my whiskers on your neck. You would kick and try to get away but I would not let you go; I would just hold you tighter. Now that you are a young lady, Daddy wants you to know that you still need hugs and I do too. As a matter of fact, studies have been done that show that people who get regular hugs are happier and healthier than people who don't.

You are developing into a beautiful young lady, and I want to warn you that it is going to be difficult for you to get a hug from a young man who will not be aroused by that hug. His hugs come from the fact that he is "turned on" by the thought of touching a young lady. It's all about hugs—but getting them the right way. You know that your daddy is a hugger and I hug everybody, but as a young man, I didn't hug a lot of girls because it would excite me so much. Now that I am older and I have you and other adopted daughters who need hugs, I can hug freely in a platonic manner.

When I say platonic, I mean with no sexual interest, like when you and your brother hug. It is very important to have someone who will give you safe hugs while you are growing up. A girl who gets healthy hugs early in life from her dad and others who love and care for her won't have the need for unhealthy hugs later on. It's best for girls to learn at an early age the proper meaning of a hug so that later on they will be able to recognize a hug that has an unhealthy meaning behind it. It's important to recognize the difference because when a boy starts to notice you and wants to hug you, his intentions will be much different.

When a dad squeezes his little girl and holds her tight, he is communicating to her that she is important—she is loved. I have made this a priority because I do not want you to be deprived of hugs and amazed by the strength of a man's arms when you get your first strong hug from another male. By hugging you, I have prepared you to not be overly impressed by the hugs you will get in the future.

I don't know if I have told you that psychologists have said that all human beings have two needs that must be met. One is the need to feel important or the need for significance. Have you ever noticed that when some people come into a room, they must speak loudly or do something that will get everyone's attention? Usually it's because these people need to feel as though they matter. So they create a moment where they can get the attention they need. I hug you because I know that you need attention; I know that you need to feel significant.

The other need that psychologists say that all human beings have is the need to feel safe or secure. When you get a hug, it gives you a feeling of security. Then you don't have to feel like you have to act out your need in public. A boy can spot a girl who suffers from a need for significance or security by observing her behavior. He can then capitalize on that need and take advantage of her.

A sincere hug signifies a relationship and lets you know that the person who hugs you has an interest in you. Therefore, hugging provides some external reinforcement by sending the message that says "You are important to me." I know a young lady who met her father for the first time when she was twenty-six years old. She said that the best thing about her relationship with him now is the fact that he gives her hugs and talks to her about men. His behavior toward her helps her feel significant.

There are many girls who have very noticeable needs, and Daddy doesn't want you to be one of them. You see the way that some girls at school let boys hug and touch them inappropriately. In most of their cases, these girls have not learned that this kind of behavior is dangerous because of where it can lead. Boys know the girls who will allow themselves to be taken advantage of and, believe me, they will go as far with a girl as she will allow. Before she knows it, a physical touch that seemed to begin innocently enough is carried too far and ends up with both of them becoming sexually aroused.

Baby, I want you to learn to ask for a hug from someone who loves you when you feel that you need one. I have learned to ask for hugs when I am having a bad day. You should always know where to get a safe hug. Remember that the proper way to hug a boy is like your dad hugs you. When a boy that you will allow to hug you approaches, prepare yourself to be in control of the hug. To keep it platonic, do these things:

1. Extend your right hand as he approaches you, and grasp his right hand.
2. While holding his right hand (using it to keep you separated), place your left hand on his right shoulder.
3. Lean your left shoulder into him touching only at the shoulders, using your right hand to keep your bodies separated. Never give him a full-body hug. He would like this but let him get his kicks somewhere else.

The Bible says, "There is a time to hug and a time not to hug" (Ecclesiastes 3:5). My goal is for you to be in touch with your feelings so when you feel that you need a hug, come and ask for one. The ability to do this is a sign of a person with a healthy sense of being. Girls always hug girls, but I want to be your main source of male hugs until you become mature enough to know who to hug and when to hug. As you get older, be sure to keep hugging friends because that can make life's difficult days more bearable.

Think About It

I. What does *platonic* mean?

_____

2. Did you receive platonic (safe) hugs when you were a little girl?
Yes___ No___ Why or why not?
Explain _____

3. Before reading this chapter, did you think about how hugging someone affects you? Yes___ No___ Why or why not? Explain _____

_____

4. Name three people whom you allow to give you safe hugs.

_____

_____

_____

5. Did you ever act out in public because you needed
attention? Yes___ No___ Why or why not?

Explain _____

If yes, do you still do it? Yes___ No___ Why or why not?

Explain _____

_____

6. Have you ever been hugged in an inappropriate way? Yes___ No___
How did it make you feel? Were you able to share the experience
with someone you trust? _____

_____

_____

7. Do you think you can actually be sure when you are being hugged inappropriately? Yes___ No___ Why or why not?

Explain _____

8. Write the three steps you should take when hugging a boy.

  1._____

  2._____

  3._____

9. Tell the truth! Does it make you feel wanted when a young man hugs you? Yes___ No___ Why or why not?

  Explain _____

10. What two needs do psychologists say that we have?

  _____

Part 2

Sex Changes Things

4)—Caution: Sexual Attraction Ahead

Here's the Deal . . .

You come home and explain to me that in biology class there was a discussion about sex and what draws the sexes toward each other. Because I am concerned about what you have heard, Dad gives you his perspective on the issue.

I ENJOY WATCHING movies about nature. There is so much to learn from the animals as we observe their interactions. Human beings and animals have a lot in common, and there is much that can be learned by studying animal life. For example, it is natural for human beings to have a sexual attraction to one another, and animals are attracted to their own kind as well.

There are times when the animals are more attracted to the opposite sex than at other times. This attraction is totally sexual in nature, and it does not mean that the animals have affection for one another. For instance, when a male elephant sees a female elephant that is ready to mate, there are chemical responses in the brain that prepare them for mating. The male elephant will chase her around for a few minutes and then they mate. So it is with humans. It is possible to see another human act on their attraction to that person sexually and not feel any love or even care for the other individual. This is commonly called having a "one-night stand."

Unfortunately, many people in our society have sexual relations in this way. There is no commitment, no love, just an activity to quench their sexual desire. I want to advise you against thinking that you have done something wrong simply by having special feelings for someone. There is nothing wrong with being attracted to a boy. In fact, as you continue to mature, you will experience sexual attractions and urges that are normal. When you have these urges, know that you are not committing a sin—you are simply being human.

The important thing is for you to realize that those sexual urges should not control you. When you find yourself sexually attracted to someone, you always want to be controlled by the Holy Spirit inside of you and not by your flesh. The Bible explains it this way: "Walk in the Spirit, and you shall not fulfill the lust of the flesh" (Galatians 5:16 NJKV). This means that you allow the Spirit of God to guide you and help you make the right decision whenever you are tempted. Following your flesh will get you into trouble every time, but listening to the Spirit of God will keep you out of trouble.

Don't think for one minute that this is not true or that it does not apply to you, because God has given you the power to understand His Word and to also live by it. You only have to believe that it is true, and He will give you the grace to conduct yourself according to His Word. Young people today are very advanced when it comes to understanding modern technology on a level that surpasses most adults. This fact convinces me that young people can also relate to God's Word with that same level of intelligence when they apply themselves and really desire to understand what God wants them to do.

It is because of a focus on Jesus Christ that you can avoid being like people in the movies or friends that you know who sleep around. The desire to have sex is real, but you can have control over it; it does not have to control you. I have been happily married for many years now, and believe me when I tell you there have been women who have crossed my path to whom I have been sexually attracted. I want you to know that, contrary to what you see in the movies, you can ignore a sexual attraction. The point is that a sexual attraction does not require action on your part.

Many young people are being misled to believe that when they become sexually aroused it is OK to "go all the way" and seek nature's solution to satisfy their feelings. But there is a problem with this thinking because nature's solution has very negative side effects for unmarried young people. It is sad to think about the many young people who fall prey to unwanted pregnancies, abortions, and sexually transmitted diseases (STDs). As a result, their casual decision to engage in sex puts their futures in real jeopardy.

There are older women who became sexually active at an early age who later on confessed that they wish they had waited. When these women were young girls, they ignored the fact that sexual activity is reserved for a marriage relationship. Even now some of them find themselves still dealing with their immature decisions of the past.

Please know that you don't have to fall for this. The effects of premarital sex cause the kind of harm that cannot always be seen with the physical eye. It makes a lasting impression on the mind and deeply affects a girl's emotions. She may not want to admit it even to herself, and may try to cover up the fact that something is bothering her, but the thoughts in one's mind can be very difficult to control and even harder to dismiss. That is why the best birth control is using self-control and exercising abstinence.

The term that sums up what you need to do to avoid the pitfalls of sexual mistakes is called "deferred gratification"! This means that you defer, or put off until later, the pleasure of sexual satisfaction. If you wait until the right time to become sexually active, the benefits will be immeasurable. When you choose to share yourself with your husband, there will be no guilt and shame in your marriage bed. If you don't wait, you will never know what sweet blessings you gave up for what amounted to a cheap thrill.

Be careful not to allow yourself to be manipulated by your normal sexual cravings. Realize that your desires are no more real and you are not being tempted more than other girls. You are normal, and with the proper discipline you can survive the test. Keep your mind on pleasing God and He will reward you. The best way to do this is to know that God will help you to do what the Scripture says, "You, Lord, give true peace to those who depend on you, because they trust you" (Isaiah 26:3). When you are trusting and depending on God, your mind is at peace and you can think clear thoughts. There is no better way to have peace in your mind than for God to give it to you. God is just waiting for you to rely on Him to give you that peace.

Let me also share with you another valuable piece of information. It takes the same discipline to stay pure after marriage as it takes to stay pure before marriage. If you cannot stay pure to God now, it will be difficult to stay faithful to your husband after marriage. One way to practice discipline and make this work for you is to be sure to do common-sense things to avoid temptation. For example, stay away from watching steamy sex scenes in movies and don't be alone with a guy.

Many young girls today are being told that it is OK to aggressively pursue boys whom they are attracted to. I want to warn you against this. I want you to know that, contrary to what you see on TV and in the movies, you can ignore the feelings brought on by sexual attraction. I have said it before and I will say it again: "You must not pursue a young man in the same manner that young men pursue you." If you don't allow yourself to be pursued by the guy, you will soon find out that you have a relationship with a weak foundation. Girls who pursue guys usually end up getting hurt in the end. It sometimes takes years, but guys who were pursued usually begin to feel trapped and will either shut down in a relationship or run away from it.

Are you strong enough to handle a sexually charged situation? The answer is no! You can't be trusted to be alone with a boy any more than I trust myself to be alone with a young beautiful woman other than my wife. Actually, it is not a matter of trust; it is a matter of common sense. A person should never put herself in a tempting situation like that. You must first guard your mind, which is where all action begins.

Baby, you are a beautiful young lady. You are beautiful on the inside and on the outside. In due time a young man will recognize you for your beauty, and he will choose to pursue you. Until then, know that your job is to set yourself apart for the glory of God. The Bible says, "A girl who has never married is busy with the Lord's work. She wants to be holy in body and spirit" (1 Corinthians 7:34).

Think About It

I. Can you rap? Try making a rap out of the following sentence: A sexual attraction does not require action.

2. What does it mean to be set apart for the glory of God?

_____

_____

3. Should you feel bad because you have a sex drive? Yes___ No___ Why? Or why not?

Explain _____

4. Has your attitude about sex been influenced by the movies? Yes___ No___ Why? Or why not?

Explain _____

5. How can we avoid being like the people in the movies who show no moral character?

_____

6. Do you allow sexual thoughts to control you? Yes___ No___ Why? Or why not?

Explain _____

_____

7. What does "deferred gratification" mean?

_____

_____

5 — Beware of Seduction

Here's the Deal . . .
You and I are watching TV together when a man begins to seduce a woman. As I turn off the TV, you state that you would never allow that to happen to you. This is the conversation that follows.

WE'RE NOT ALWAYS as strong as we think we are. Any of us could do anything in the right circumstances. This is especially true as it relates to sex, romance, and seduction. How many young girls have said that they would never engage in intimate activities with a guy and then become pregnant? The power of seduction can be very deceiving. It takes real determination not to fall into the trap because before you know it, you can be in its grasp.

On the other hand, being seduced by the right person at the right time in the right place is a truly wonderful experience. I met my wife, dated her, and married her. Then she eventually allowed me to seduce her. The seduction began when I first met her and culminated on our honeymoon. Did you notice that I said that she let me? Well, that is the truth. Now we are deeper in love than ever before, and seduction has taken on a whole new dimension. She actually seduces me when she walks into a room. So seduction can be good, and seduction has more aspects than the well-known sexual aspect.

Let's look at some things you need to consider as we discuss seduction. When you are in the presence of someone who wants to seduce you, you should immediately guard your mind.

You must maintain mental control at all times.

Seduction can only happen when your mind cooperates with the person who is attempting to seduce you. The seducer knows that if he can get you to concentrate on what he is concentrating on then he will be successful. The idea is that he wants you to stop thinking about protecting yourself from what can happen and begin thinking about what he is thinking about—and that is seducing you.

Remember that all sexual activity begins as a thought. The mind considers the action first, and then the feelings and emotions take over. So if you keep your thoughts on preventing someone else's will from taking control of your own, you have a much better chance to make the situation go in the direction that you want it to go.

You must understand your response to seduction.

People enjoy being seduced because:

1. It makes them feel important.
2. It gives a false sense of self-esteem.
3. There is a sense of safety when someone more powerful than you is temporarily in control.

Today's society is fascinated by seduction and encourages it. It is a strange fact that being seduced is considered fun. People are going out of their way to get seduced, even paying others to seduce them. To be seduced is to allow your interest in a person, place, or thing to increase as you think about it or look at it. Almost every commercial that I can think of has a person in it who has lost control because of a hamburger, car, vacation, cash money, or a woman. So seduction is not only sexual, but it can apply to any desire or passion.

As girls begin to develop physically, it is normal to feel attracted to boys, which by itself is not wrong. But it becomes dangerous when a young lady's curiosity takes her attraction to a boy to the next level by seducing him into sexual activity. A girl who constantly flirts can easily stir up a boy's natural desire for sex. You probably know girls who have already lost their virginity because of their careless behavior toward sex. More often than not, they end up regretting the fact that they gave in to a boy's advances. Excuses such as finding out about sex too late and saying she just didn't know can turn into sad news because a girl can't take back her virginity once she has given it away.

It's so crucial to play it smart when it comes to seduction. When a person chooses not to continue to think about another person, place, or thing that interests them, the seductive control is broken. This is why it is so important not to fill your mind with dirty images of people being seduced. When you put it in your mind, the Enemy will remind you of it over and over again. Some people may call you square for not watching every dirty movie that comes out, but I say that you are wise not to pollute your mind with obscene material. Remember, you do have a choice in what you allow your mind to concentrate on. It is no mystery where our thoughts should focus; we know the Bible tells us to "think about the things that are true and honorable and right and pure and beautiful and respected" (Philippians 4:8).

Why do people go to such great extremes to be seduced? Well, many of them have low self-esteem, and their self-esteem is boosted when another person takes an interest in them. Unfortunately, many young girls do not have a father figure in their lives, and they enjoy the interest that some guy is giving them.

You must understand the male mind as it relates to seduction. Men are born with the instinct to conquer and subdue. God placed this desire in males when He made man, as described in Genesis 1:28, "God blessed them and said, 'Have many children and grow in number. Fill the earth and be its master.'"

This dominate nature is generally a part of most boys' attitude toward their love interests. As immature young men they feel that it is manly to use the art of persuasion, which they call their "rap." This is how they bring a girl under their influence. It is only the ones who grow into mature men who learn how to relate to females in a loving manner. In this way they recognize that a mutual agreement to become intimate is the best way to approach women with the subject of intimacy.

Then there is the lust factor that must be considered. Men are different than women as it relates to sexual pressure. Young men have physical pressure that needs to be released. That is not the case with females, which explains why young girls cannot understand the pressure boys put on them to have sex. As far as you are concerned, his need to release pressure is his personal problem, but you should never forget that it is part of his motivation for "rapping" to you.

Consider how boys view you. In most cases, girls have no clue how sexually charged boys are and how God has prepared them for sexual activity at an early age. As a result of this, boys think about sex a large part of the day. You can help them by acting and dressing modestly while you are around them. If you don't know what modest behavior is, imagine that your dad and your pastor are watching you interact with the boy. The way you would behave then would be considered modest behavior.

Seduction is nothing to play with. Once you are married, you can seduce your husband with your eyes, elegance, enchantments, and all that God has given you. Until then, when you notice seduction happening in life or on TV, turn it off just like Dad turned the TV off.

Think About It

1. Do you watch movies that have a lot of seductive scenes in them? Yes___ No___ Why or why not?

Explain _____

2. Why do you think people like to watch so much sex on TV?

_____

3. Do you flirt with boys? Yes___ No___ Why or why not?

Explain _____

4. Do you know how to control your thoughts when it comes to boys? Yes___ No___

Explain _____

5. Do you watch TV programs that have a lot of sex scenes or do you turn it off or leave the room?_____ Why or why not?

Explain _____

6. Has a boy ever tried to seduce you? Yes___ No___

Explain _____

7. What does the Enemy do when you allow bad images to enter into your mind?_____

8. Should you feel bad because you have a sex drive? Yes___ No___ Why or why not?

Explain _____

9. Has your attitude about sex been influenced by movies and TV programs? Yes___ No___

Explain _____

6)—Babies Makin' Babies

Here's the Deal . . .

Your best friend is fifteen and has found out that she is pregnant. Because she believes that abortion is murder, she chooses to have the child even though she knows that it will be very difficult for her. This is what your dad has to say to you as you discuss this issue with him.

BABY, I KNOW that this is a rough time for you and your friend. Just as you are, I am deeply concerned for her and her baby. I am glad that she did not choose to abort the child. However, she has a life-changing decision to make as she decides whether to keep the baby or put the child up for adoption.

Childbirth is a onetime act that changes the world forever. No matter what happened, when a baby is brought into this world, neither the mother nor the world will ever be the same. Once life has been created, that life will exist forever—even if it is aborted. This is why having a child is both a physical and sacred responsibility. You need to know that sex is a sacred act.

Listen to how the psalmist expresses his feelings to God about his conception and development in his mother's womb,

"You made my whole being; you formed me in my mother's body. I praise you because you made me in an amazing and wonderful way. What you have done is wonderful. I know this very well. You saw my bones being formed as I took shape in my mother's body. When I was put together there, you saw my body as it was formed. All the days planned for me were written in your book before I was one day old" (Psalm 139:13–16).

I want to remind you that I was there when you took your first breath. It was a beautiful sight. It was interesting to me how you had to fight to begin life. I was amazed at how you and your mother struggled during the birth process.

I also want you to know that I am looking forward to the day when you and your future husband can announce that you are expecting. That's going to be a tremendous joy for me and your mother. Even though being a grandparent will be a wonderful thing, I want you to know that I can wait until the time is right.

Baby, Daddy wants you to know that you don't have to have a baby to feel loved. I have known of countless young ladies who had babies just because they felt that they needed someone to love them. I know that it gives a young woman a wonderful sense of self-worth to bring a life into this world, but if it is done prematurely or without the proper support of a loving husband, then caring for a baby can be a terrible burden. A young lady must reach a certain level of maturity to raise a child correctly.

The truth of the matter is that a person is not fit to be a parent until they have become mature enough to understand their own strengths and weaknesses and really know what they are capable of doing. Before a young lady thinks of becoming a mother, she should know how she will react in certain situations. For example, does she give up easily when something gets too hard for her to deal with? Or does she keep pressing on until she has done everything she is expected to do?

The possibility of having a baby points to the serious nature of sex. As a result, human beings should behave responsibly when we put ourselves in the situation where pregnancy can occur. Unfortunately, too often a lack of love between two prospective parents plays a part when babies are conceived. I also feel that immaturity plays a major role too. A characteristic of an immature person is one who will do something without considering the consequences.

Remember that time you stood up in the front seat of the car and took the car out of gear, causing it to roll backward across the street? If you had understood the consequences, I am sure you would not have taken such a risk. Children might be very familiar with the concept of riding in a car, but they do not understand its potential for destruction when they take chances and use it in an improper way.

It is the same way when young people mature sexually. Their bodies have a capacity for adult activities that they cannot fully understand or handle yet. They need to know that even though they are not ready for it to happen, their bodies have the potential to produce life. Further proof of immaturity is when some young people make a baby as a result of a dare. Someone challenges them or they are in a pressure situation, and they decide to take a chance. I hope you know that it only takes one sexual encounter (no matter how brief) to become pregnant. Contrary to a popular notion, it really can happen the first time.

Babies makin' babies really comes down to an issue of the heart for a young lady who is considering having a baby to satisfy her need for love. But what she should know is that getting pregnant before she is truly ready is definitely not the answer. A baby alone cannot fulfill anyone's need. In fact, the mother will wind up giving more love than she can receive from a newborn baby.

Before she knows it, a girl who is looking for a way to fill a void in her life is presented with an opportunity in the form of a guy who is interested in her. She then decides to take a chance on love by getting pregnant. The boy is more than likely going to be very willing to accommodate her and engage in sex with her. But, believe me, the average boy is not interested in having sex for the same reason as a girl who thinks she wants a baby. Boys have a different motive for getting intimately involved with girls. His intention and desire are going to be purely physical, whereas the girl is looking to fulfill an emotional need. This is what you could call a "perfect storm." Something very risky is just waiting to happen. And suddenly, a simple act of sex has taken place that will play a big part in the girl's destiny.

Unfortunately, this girl has confused her longing for love with wanting to have a baby who will love her and satisfy her need in a way that she feels no one else can. Human beings have a need to feel important, and they also have a need to be needed. Yes, the baby will belong to her, and no one can take that away from her. So she decides that she is ready to have a baby whose primary reason for existence will be to respond to her need while at the same time she is caring for the needs of the child.

This sounds simple enough. But the problem is that this thinking is not completely balanced. She is focusing only on the "pretty" side of having a baby. The idea just won't hold up because she wants something good to happen—but for the wrong reason. This tiny little infant who is so fragile and cute is not merely going to give her the love that she craves. In reality, this bundle of joy is also going to give her many sleepless nights when the baby seems to cry nonstop for no apparent reason. Then too she will experience some other extremely frustrating times. Once the baby is fed and diapered, she will be at her wit's end trying to figure out what more the baby could possibly want or need.

To make matters even worse, the young lady has to get up early in the morning and get the little one and herself ready to take the baby to a sitter while she goes on to school and/or work. That means even less time she has to spend with the child whom she thought would be the answer to her problem. Instead of satisfying her hunger for love, the baby seems to show very little gratitude for anything this new mom tries to do. After all, the baby can't say thank you or show any other form of appreciation except maybe an occasional smile or giggle.

But is that really enough to make up for all the trouble this young mom has to endure? Of course, I'm talking about the sleepless nights and the lack of a social life; that vanished when the baby arrived. No more going out to parties and just hanging out with friends. Freedom to do what she wants when she wants is now a thing of the past—it's history. The baby's needs must always come first, and babies definitely have lots of needs.

Far too many girls have been down that road and could tell you that it's a hard reality for a young girl to face. I know that this is straight talk, but I want you to realize the seriousness of this matter. Perhaps you haven't thought of it this way before, but nevertheless, this is a harsh reality that many young unwed mothers face today.

Baby, with a made-up mind and the support of your family, our church family, and your closest friends, I am sure that you can resist the temptation to experiment with having sex—something that could change your life forever. I am here for you when you need to talk.

Think About It

1. Do you have a baby or have any friends who have a baby? Yes___ No___ Why? Or why not?

   Explain _____

2. Would you have an abortion if you were pregnant? Yes___ No___ Why? Or why not?

   Explain _____

   Do you think that abortion is murder? Yes___ No___ Why? Or why not?

   Explain _____

3. If you had a baby, who would feed, clothe, and give you and your child a home?

   _____

4. Do you understand that from God's perspective a baby in the womb is just as complete as a baby in your lap? Yes___ No___ Why? Or why not?

   Explain _____

5. Having a baby is both a physical and a _____ responsibility.

6. How do you think having good self-esteem will keep you from getting pregnant?

   _____

7. Do you think that a young lady should have the moral, emotional, and financial support of a husband before she has a baby? Yes___ No___ Why? Or why not?

   Explain _____

7 — The Romance Road

BABY, DADDY wants to talk to you about romance. Romance is a wonderful thing. It is one of the pleasures that God has given men and women to be shared together. However, I feel that I should caution you because romance can be a girl's weakness—and guys know it. When I dated your momma, I romanced her. I did the flowers, long walks, talks for hours, and dinners by candlelight.

You need to be mindful of the fact that guys will play you, and they will play the part of the romantic angel in an effort to win you over. Girls love romance but they become so frustrated when many guys do not continue to be romantic after they have won their hearts. So I want you to be aware that there may be a lot of romance in the beginning of the relationship, but the real test for romance is how long it will continue after the relationship gets going.

So before you make a quick decision to become involved with a guy, please remember to think ahead of the situation and not just in the moment. This will help you avoid crossing the line between innocent romance and premarital sex. Although they should not be engaging in sexual intimacy, many young people overlook God's reason for having sex and go ahead and get involved anyway. But what some girls fail to consider is whether the guy will be there for her if she happens to get pregnant. Even so, let's say that he does commit himself to her and the baby; she has potentially robbed herself of what her future could be like had she put her future and her best interests first.

Romance is hard work for most men, but God made women in a way that they readily respond to romance. The problem is that men don't respond to romance the same way that women do. While the guy is romancing you, he is not thinking about romance as much as you are. He is thinking about the physical aspect of the relationship. He gets excited about how you look, what you wear, how you smell, and the possibility that one day soon he may be intimate with you. His motives may be pure or they may be selfish. The bottom line is that romance will be the road that he takes to get to your heart. Be careful when guys try to romance you.

While on the road of romance, be sure to observe the posted road signs. It is important for you to make sure that you do not allow the young man to violate the rules of the road.

1. You must not allow him to exceed the speed limit. By this I mean that if you meet him this week, you should not be spending time at his house next week. If you just met him this week, you should not be spending all day Saturday with him. If you just met him this week, don't even think that you are in love with him. If you just met him this week, he can't possibly be more than an acquaintance or a casual friend. Don't rush the relationship. If he is for you, he won't go anywhere, nor will anyone take him from you. Don't allow him to exceed the speed limit. Relationships that progress too rapidly often fail. Remember that no matter how romantic you feel, don't rush!

2. Make him stay in his lane. When you are with a boy, there is a line that he should not cross. If you are at a stage of only holding hands, then that is his lane and he should stay in it. If you have decided that it's OK to hug (and by the way, you should decide when to hug and not just let it happen), then that becomes the lane that he is to stay in. Keep in mind that you are on a two-lane road with cars in the other lane going in the opposite direction, so to wander off course can be deadly.

Please remember and use the promise ring that I placed on your finger. Always hold it up to him and remind him that you belong to your dad until that day when the promise ring is replaced with a wedding ring. Never let a guy pressure you! Remember that if a man wants sex without demonstrating commitment, he just wants sex.

3. Come to a complete stop at all stoplights and stop signs.
If there is a problem stopping the premature progression of intimacy, meaning if he wants to have sex or even kiss and hug too much—then it is time to get off of the road. If you allow him to run stop signs, there is an immediate danger to your future well-being. When stop signs are run, it is evidence that you are possibly being viewed as a plaything or a boy's toy. It is a lie when a boy tells you that he can't stop! It is a lie if you tell yourself that you can't stop! Get up from wherever you are and start walking—that will put an end to it!

4. Maintain a full tank of fuel for the journey.
Your relationship with God and your spiritual disciplines (good habits) should be maintained, if not increased while on the romance road. Bible reading and prayer will give you the right perspective. Rule number one: When you are in love, you don't think as clearly as you do at other times. As a result of this natural tendency, it becomes necessary to be equipped with Scriptures that you can repeat and hold on to for times like this.

Here are some verses for you to memorize:

> "I have taken your words to heart so I would not sin against you" (Psalm 119:11).
>
> "The only temptation that has come to you is that which everyone has. But you can trust God, who will not permit you to be tempted more than you can stand. But when you are tempted, he will also give you a way to escape so that you will be able to stand it" (1 Corinthians 10:13).
>
> "Happy are those who don't listen to the wicked, who don't go where sinners go, who don't do what evil people do" (Psalm 1:1).

5. Keep emergency supplies on hand at all times.
No! I'm not talking about condoms. Frequently when young people are on the

romance road, they will stop doing other things, like talking to their parents and close friends about how the relationship is going. Your trusted friends and family can provide a clear viewpoint for you when you begin your journey down the road of romance. You should never travel without your safety kit of wisdom and perspective that is available from loved ones.

6. Consider counsel very wisely. It is dangerous to take advice from friends your age. The reason is that they don't have enough life experience to really give you good advice. You can learn a lot from the people you know who have been your age, tried what you are doing, grew up, and found out the results of their actions. This is called experience. Experience is a great teacher, but it can use you up in the process of teaching you—so learn as much as you can from other people's experiences. The Word of God is the best teacher, and obedience to the Word is the best protector.

Girls your age who have made mistakes can only tell you from experience about the immediate pain that has resulted from their mistake. They cannot tell you about the pain involved many years into the future because they haven't lived through that yet themselves. This is the problem with getting advice from people your own age.

I recently accompanied a lady who went to visit her son in jail. She shared with me that many years ago she was in love and against all of her family's and friends' advice, she stayed with this man and was intimate with him. They had a child whom she tried to raise by herself. Twenty years later she found herself still dealing with the results of that mistake she made when she was young.

So when you are thinking about allowing some guy to romance you, think again. Before you allow him to take you down that road, make up your mind that you're not going to go so far that you will be sorry later on. A baby is not a toy that can be discarded when you get bored with it. A child is a human life just like you are, with feelings, needs, hurts, and emotions too. Children do not ask to come into this world, but they deserve every opportunity to have a good life once they are here. Are you ready for the awesome responsibility that all of this would bring into your life? Think hard and consider all of these factors before your answer.

Yes, romance is a wonderful experience, but if you are not careful, you can very easily make some life-altering mistakes as you go along. Godly counsel, prayer, and some much-needed discipline will help you make it safely down that exciting but potentially dangerous road.

Think About It

1. Do you read romance novels? Yes___ No___ Do you watch romantic movies? Yes___ No___ Why? Or why not?

   Explain _____

2. Does your imagination run away with romantic thoughts? Yes___ No___ Why? Or why not?

   Explain _____

   _____

3. Do you think that girls are more vulnerable to romance than boys? Yes___ No___ Why? Or why not?

   Explain _____

   _____

4. What road will boys take to get to your heart?_____

5. In most cases, as the relationship progresses, the level of romance increases _____ or decreases _____? Why? Or why not?

   Explain _____

6. Under the section that talks about observing posted road signs, there are six signs that you need to watch out for. List the two signs that you feel are most important to you and briefly tell why.

   _____

   _____

   _____

7. Name the family members and friends whom you will talk with and listen to when you think you're ready to become romantically involved.

   _____

   _____

Part 3

Enjoy Being a Girl

8)—You're Not Going Out of THIS House Looking Like That!

Here's the Deal . . .

It is a hot Saturday morning in June. You are fourteen years old and you come down the stairs wearing some Daisy Duke shorts and a cutoff T-shirt that shows your belly button. Here is your dad's response.

BABY, DADDY wants you to know one thing—and that is, if you think that you are going out of this house looking like that, I want you to think again. I feel very strongly about the matter. So if you try to walk out of this house looking like that, I'll have to stop you.

I want you to consider the fact that most girls have no idea what they do to boys and to themselves when they walk around wearing very short cutoff jeans and their belly buttons exposed. My momma would say that your belly button is stickin' out. I know what you are going to say but you must understand. I feel so strongly about this because I know what the young men are going to think when they see you dressed like that!

I know how distracting it is. And since you thought that it was OK to dress like that, there are at least three things that you obviously do not understand:

1. What happens to a young man's mind when he
   sees you dressed like that

2. The amount of respect you lose when young men see you dressed
   like that

3. How they feel about your father and family
   members when they see you dressed like that

I don't care how nice the young man is; if he has a masculine nature, then he is a typical male. That means he will be unnecessarily aroused when you expose parts of your body that should be covered. Young men can get excited about anything they see. Sometimes even a girl's elbow can be terribly sexy to a young man because of where his mind is at that time. You can be dressed in an old sweat suit and minding your own business, but a guy can see something sexy in that apparel too. I am not trying to restrict your freedom, but I am trying to protect your reputation and purity.

Moderate dress could be defined as: "Dress that covers body parts that are only to be exposed when men and women are intimate." Women have body parts that should only be seen by their husbands in their bedrooms. When these parts or the edges of these parts are seen in public, this is definitely immodest dress. When you show the edges of your body parts, it is an invitation for the man's eyes to focus on the edges and for his mind to imagine the rest. As your dad, I don't want you to even show the edges of your private parts.

In some cultures, women are required to cover themselves completely. One of the reasons this is done is because the men don't want to be tempted to think lustful thoughts by seeing a woman's body, so women are commanded to cover everything. Of course I am not going to that extreme, but the way you are dressed right now is really the other extreme.

One of the ways a man judges a woman is by the way she dresses. I have seen women dress like a prostitute and get angry when a man talked to them like they are one. The amount of respect that a guy will give you will be determined partly by the way you dress. Young men will judge your need for love and attention by the way you dress. They will assess your relationship with your father by the way you dress. As a matter of fact, if I let you go out of this house looking like that, the young men in the neighborhood will think that I am the biggest fool in the community! You're not going out of this house lookin' like that!

Baby, you are a very smart young lady, but with all of your intelligence it is impossible for you to think like a man. Daddy is trying to hip you to how a man thinks. I am trying to show you why you should not provoke men to think lustful thoughts by dressing in an offensive way. The apostle Peter put this subject into clear terms when he said, "It is not fancy hair, gold jewelry, or fine clothes that should make you beautiful. No, your beauty should come from within you—the beauty of a gentle and quiet spirit that will never be destroyed and is very precious to God" (1 Peter 3:3-4).

You never have to worry about attracting fine, sensible young men because not only does your beauty shine from within you, but your physical beauty speaks for itself. So there is no reason for you to think that you must wear revealing clothes. Instead you should focus on wearing only moderate clothing that allows your true beauty to shine through.

Men are stimulated by what they see. So out of respect for their visual weaknesses and as a courtesy to them, wise women choose to be modest in their dress. They know that men are tempted to look when women dress in a tempting manner. They know that this draws the wrong type of attention, so they try to avoid attracting that type of attention to themselves. Also, women should dress modestly when they go to church because it is hard for brothers to think about God when a sister walks into church wearing a miniskirt.

Throughout history, women who sought men's attention dressed a certain way. We see in these two examples from Scripture that women have always given messages by the clothes they wear.

> "She approached him, saucy and pert, and dressed seductively. She was the brash, coarse type, seen often in the streets and markets, soliciting at every corner for men to be her lovers" (Proverbs 7:10-12 TLB).
>
> "Women [and girls] should wear proper clothes that show respect and self-control" (1 Timothy 2:9).

These are extremely opposite approaches for females to take: the first one clearly has the wrong intention, and the second is the right choice because it will send the right message about who you are. Many young ladies don't understand how their clothing affects men until they are in their thirties or fourties. Even today I won't let your mom wear a short, short dress because she is married. When you expose body parts, you get a boy's attention. The problem with getting a man's attention through provocative dressing is that you draw the attention of many undesirable and even some "sick-in-the-head" men. Fathers know how sick other men's minds can be.

Modest dress, on the other hand, will still get the attention of intelligent, thinking men. When you dress modestly you automatically eliminate a whole category of lowlife scum that would otherwise be attracted to you. Your dad is all man, and believe me, I know what I am talking about.

Well—what will it be? Are you going to change clothes without an argument? I draw the line right here. Because I love you, you will not go out of this house dressed like that.

Think About It

I. Would you change your clothes if your dad or pastor asked you to? Yes___ No___ Why? Or why not?

Explain _____

2. Dad said there were at least three things you do not understand when you dress provocatively. Read them again.

3. Do you like to excite young men by dressing provocatively? Yes___ No___ Why? Or why not?

Explain _____

Do you consider tight jeans provocative? Yes___ No___ Do you consider Daisy Duke shorts provocative? Yes___ No___

4. Do any adults challenge the way you dress?

_____

5. Do you think about your motives when you dress? Yes___ No___ Why? Or why not?

Explain _____

6. Dad states that most girls don't understand how their dress affects men until they are in their _____. Do you think some girls understand this earlier in life? Yes___ No___

7. Dressing in provocative clothes draws healthy men, but it also draws _____.

8. Do you know girls who dress for the sole purpose of provoking men? Yes___ No___

9. Did you know that men are more visually stimulated than women? Yes___ No___

IO. Write your own definition of modest dress. Modest dress is

_____.

9)—Don't Act Like a Man

BABY, YOU WILL never attract a guy by acting like a man. You will not get a guy by talking, walking, thinking, cursing, or fighting like a man. Not too long ago, I was on the Quad (the grassy area in the middle of the campus) of the University of Illinois during what is called Quad Day. This is a festive time when all of the students gather and there are displays and shows to be seen. A friend of mine was there with his two small children enjoying the festivities when twenty feet away from where he was standing, two young college girls got into a fight. I did not see it, but my friend stated that they grabbed each other around the neck and went down to the ground like two men. He said that when they hit the ground, he felt the ground shake twenty feet from where they were.

What was most distressing about the whole event was that they were fighting over a man. So you say that you would never fight over a man? Well, what would you fight over? There is an attitude that is becoming very popular among young ladies in which they feel that they must be as tough or tougher than the guys that they want to hang out with. These unfortunate young women did not realize how their behavior made a negative impression on those who saw them. The Bible says, "Foolishness is like a loud woman; she does not have wisdom or knowledge" (Proverbs 9:13). In dealing with that situation, they needed to demonstrate their intelligence a whole lot more than they needed the guy they were fighting over.

Baby, I want you to know that real men do not appreciate that type of behavior. The more you mature, the more you will realize that guys are most attracted to young ladies who are comfortable with their feminity. Real men are turned off by a young lady who tries to be as tough as a man. There is no need for two men in the relationship. I once had a girlfriend tell me that she would not have a man whose hair was prettier than hers. Well, men don't like women who are tougher, meaner, and more masculine than they are.

Some of the reasons young women will act like a man are:

1. She has not been taught to be feminine. Generally, feminine characteristics are passed on from a mature woman to a younger woman. But in some circumstances young girls have not been taught how to be feminine. By the same principle, there are boys who act feminine because they are surrounded by their mothers and other women, and no man is present to model masculine behavior for them. It is OK if a girl doesn't know how to be feminine, but it is not OK to stay that way. She needs an older, graceful woman to teach her the social graces. Then she can practice what has been modeled for her and what she has been taught.

2. She has been abandoned and left to find her own way. Unfortunately many young girls have been virtually abandoned as it relates to being taught the finer points of life. Because of their own struggles, many mothers leave their daughters to find their way through life on their own. It is no longer a priority for many parents to take the time to teach young ladies how to sit, walk, and act like a lady. Usually, if it is not important to Mom, it won't be important to her daughter.

3. She is mean-spirited. Some girls are just plain mean. It is a fact that all behavior is motivated or caused by something. In other words, there is a reason why a girl behaves the way that she does. Most mean people are angry at someone, and they display that pain to everyone they meet. In order for mean people to live a happy and healthy life, it is important to discover what has made them bitter and seek to resolve those issues. Girls who have a habit of being mean fear having the appearance of weakness. Sadly, they feel it is necessary to put up a mean front to protect themselves. They determine early in life that they do not want to be on the losing side of any argument. Having a mean attitude toward life will not get a young lady very far. The Bible says that "a kind woman gets respect" (Proverbs 11:16).

4. She may be starved for love and panics at the thought of losing her boyfriend. It is very sad when a young lady dreads the thought of losing her boyfriend to the point where she would be totally lost without him. It is normal to be hurt and sad, but it tells a lot about her if she comes totally unglued when she finds out that she and her boyfriend are breaking up. It could be that she is starved for love or her self-esteem is so low that she needs a guy to give some meaning to her life. This is why I don't recommend that young ladies listen to those silly love songs that talk about dying if a boyfriend leaves. These songs are negative at their core and encourage depression over a breakup.

There are additional reasons why girls act manly, but in the final analysis, you need to look at yourself to make sure that you are not acting that way. It is a little-known fact that a young lady can command respect and attention by the way she walks into a room. The act of sitting in a chair, when done gracefully, will cause men to pay attention. The way you hold or turn your head says a lot about your grace and style. Social graces can be a part of your life without you being labeled a "square." In the end, the girls who act like boys are the squares who will be out of place as they get older.

Think About It

I. Are you a girl who likes to dress and act manly? Yes___ No___ Why? Or why not?

Explain _____

2. Do you know girls who like to fight and act manly? Yes___ No___

3. Who teaches you to be feminine? _____

4. Which do you feel wise boys like, manly girls or feminine girls?

_____

5. Why do you feel that so many girls these days act manly?

_____

6. Find and complete this sentence: Real men are turned _____

_____.

7. Would you date a guy whose hair is prettier than yours? Yes___ No___ Why? Or why not?

Explain _____

8. Why do you feel so many girls are mean today?

_____

9. Do you feel that you have to be a stereotypically pretty girl to act feminine? Yes___ No___ Why? Or why not?

Explain _____

10)—Baby, Daddy Wants You to Keep a Pure Mouth

Here's the Deal . . .

While sitting and watching TV together, a female rapper comes on the tube. After tolerating a few minutes of her vulgar mouth and inappropriate dress, your dad turns to you and says:

AS A MAN, there is nothing more repulsive than a woman with a foul mouth (yuck!). It has always turned me off and now that I am older, it turns me off, even more. It is very unfortunate that so many young girls feel that they profit in some way by talking like that. The fact of the matter is that they are seen as losers by thinking men. If you don't talk and act like you deserve respect, then you can't expect anyone to give it to you.

When immature men hear you talk like that, they will do one of several things:

I. They will see you as a lowlife hood rat and decide to use you as a disposable toy for a while. Because they have no respect for you, they will promise you the world but will deliver only pain. When girls buy into the thinking that talking vulgar is all good, they are sadly underestimating their personal value. The bottom line is: You really need to watch what you say and how you say it.

2. They will see you as a challenge and compete with you to see who can be the best at talking in vulgar language. Usually, a guy can beat a girl at being vulgar because he is stronger and can resort to physical violence to make his point if necessary.

3. They will be totally turned off by your mouth and avoid you like the plague. It is a terrible mistake when young women fall for the trap of thinking that to be equal or better than a guy is to beat him at his own game. This is an awful situation for a girl to find herself in. You can never beat a boy at his own game, but you can render him helpless when you force him to play God's game. I know that this advice goes against what you see on TV and in society, but take it from a man; it works!

The approach that God intends for girls to use with boys is the attitude of meekness, hooked up to godliness. Meekness means using gentleness and having a sweet attitude. You don't go off on a boy with one hand on your hip, rolling your head around on your neck, and pointing your finger in his face talking dirty language. Guys either laugh at or ignore that type of behavior. Instead of impressing boys, they will form a low opinion of girls who have bad language habits. Remember, your choice of language either shows intelligence on your part or a lack of it.

By nature, guys can be good at being lowdown, nasty, and dirty. When a girl decides to go that way, she is playing the guy at his strongest point. When the girl plays the role that God has designated that she play, meekness hooked up with godliness, the guy becomes helpless. This is why historically women have been given credit for taming men. When a man decided to get married, people would say: "Oh, he's settling down."

Men do not naturally know how to respond to meekness. It makes them step back and think. They can't hit it; and it's inappropriate to yell at it. As a matter of fact, if the man responds with anything other than kindness, he is made to look like a fool. Take it from me; if you relate to a guy with meekness and goodness, you will have a greater influence on him than by using a sharp, foul tongue. Proverbs 15:1 reminds us, "A gentle answer will calm a person's anger, but an unkind answer will cause more anger." Try this and see how situations work out better this way.

Another problem with having a foul mouth is when you decide to act and talk sweetly, the brother remembers that just recently you were cursing with the same mouth that you are now using to be sweet. This will cause him to think that you are a hypocrite and look at you with suspicion. The apostle James explained it this way, "People can tame every kind of wild animal, bird, reptile, and fish, and they have tamed them, but no one can tame the tongue. It is wild and evil and full of deadly poison. We use our tongues to praise our Lord and Father, but then we curse people, whom God made like himself. Praises and curses come from the same mouth! My brothers and sisters, this should not happen" (James 3:7–10).

When you talk with the same sweet tongue all of the time, a reasonable man will learn to rest in your consistency. On the other hand, when you do need to tell the guy off, do it lovingly with a soft, firm voice and then stick to what you have said. There is no need to yell and curse. You are most effective and powerful when your mouth is a source of sweet words. Make it your goal to develop the discipline not to allow your own mouth to be used against you. Learn how to control your tongue and use gentle, powerful words that will work on your behalf. The Word of God is the greatest teacher: "When you talk, do not say harmful things, but say what people need—words that will help others become stronger" (Ephesians 4:29).

Think About It

1. Have you ever cursed at boys? Yes___ No___ Have you ever been tempted to curse at boys? Yes___ No___ Why? Or why not?

   Explain _____

2. Do you listen to rappers who curse and say foul words? Yes___ No___ If yes, have you memorized any of their negative lyrics? Yes___ No___

3. List the three possible responses that boys will have to your cursing:

   1. _____

      _____

   2. _____

      _____

   3. _____

      _____

4. Do you feel that you could be more vulgar than a boy? Yes___ No___ Do you want to be? Yes___ No___ Do you hang out with people who are impressed by foul language? Yes___ No___ Why? Or why not?

   Explain _____

5. How do you feel about a girl who is meek in her behavior?_____ _____ Why is meekness a powerful quality for a girl to have?

   _____

6. What is the terrible trap that girls should seek to avoid falling into?

   _____

7. What is the approach that God has designed for a girl to take as she relates to boys? _____

8. Do you yell at boys when you get angry? Yes___ No___ Why? Or why not?

   Explain _____
   If you do yell at them, do you know that you are providing a source of free entertainment for them? Yes___ No___

11)—I Don't Want You Hanging Out Everywhere

Here's the Deal . . .

I drove by the football practice the other day, and one of your friends was there looking through the fence and yelling at the players. When I saw this, I was sad for her because she doesn't realize how this makes her look. After I observed how your friend hangs out, I feel that we need to have this discussion.

BABY, BE CAREFUL where you hang out. When you hang out in the wrong places, you send a message to the boys who are there. You must understand that boys are always looking for a clue about what you are thinking or what kind of girl you are. Girls who can be found in questionable places such as at parties, dances, or clubs where drinking and illegal activity is taking place are perceived by guys as looking to have a good time. The only problem is that the good time that they will have will be from a negative perspective. By that I mean that you are sending the message that you are ready to "get down."

People who socialize at places where alcohol and drugs are being consumed are there to cut loose, get loose, and throw off restraint. Restraint . . . I like that word. It means something that holds you back from going all the way in any area of life. You should use restraint when you talk, walk, spend money, and have fun. Parties and dances where alcohol is served are places where people go to throw off all restraint. Proverbs 4:14–15 issues a warning that should not be ignored, "Don't follow the ways of the wicked; don't do what evil people do. Avoid their ways, and don't follow them. Stay away from them and keep on going."

On the other hand, church is where people go each Sunday to put on restraint. You are reminded in church that God owns your body and you can't do anything that you want to do with it. Husbands are reminded to love their wives and to give them honor and respect. We are told to be wise with money and many other things that please God. Don't go to places that encourage you to throw off restraint. You need to think about the places that you go, because your presence in those places speaks to the guys around you. Remember that fools' faces are seen in foolish places.

Now, if you feel that you can go someplace and not adapt to the way of thinking of those around you, you are partially right. I can hear you thinking: *Just because I go there does not mean that I have to act like they act.* This is partly true, but if you stay around the wrong type of environment long enough, you will be negatively affected. The guys who go to parties and clubs to drink and socialize will not approach you according to the way that you are thinking. Instead they will treat you according to the thinking of the negative environment that you are in. So wherever you happen to be—at the party, dance, or club—they will come to you with that mind-set.

Now, the reverse is also true. There are girls who go to church and are perceived by the guys there as if they are good Christian young ladies when that is not always the case. All I am trying to do is to get you to see that it is very important to pay close attention to where you go and how you will be viewed while you are there.

You know that as a married man I don't go to bars for singles. I don't go to bars at all because the people there don't think like I think, and if I hang with them their thinking will rub off on me. I also don't hang out with divorced men because I want to stay married, and the lifestyle of divorced men could influence me. Now, if I have to be careful where and with whom I hang out, then what about you? Let me say it this way: if I can't go everywhere and keep my life together, what makes you think that you can?

With this in mind, you can see why you and I need to have these discussions about the parties that you can and cannot attend. I am not condemning all parties, but I am saying that the wrong parties are merely places where players come to play, and when nice girls play they usually get hurt because they don't understand the rules.

Let me say this while I'm talking about it. A player is a person who needs to grow up. Playing is for kids. So don't fall for the temptation to play or become a player. You will get burned and end up with a negative attitude. Out of all the players in my generation, I cannot think of one who did not end up with great pain in their lives.

You should never play a dice game with the Devil because you will lose. You can't go on *his* turf and play by *your* rules. You will eventually be forced to play by his rules, and his rules are not fair. Hanging out in places that are inappropriate will only lead to trouble for a nice girl like you. Watch your step. Before you give in to the temptation to venture into places that appear harmful, remember what the Word of God says and "test everything. Keep what is good, and stay away from everything that is evil" (1 Thessalonians 5:21–22).

Do you remember when you wanted to go to a house party and I told you that you could not go? I began to ask questions: Whose house is it? What kind of house is it? Do they go to church? You must be careful whose house you go into because you do not know what is inside the house. It is a spiritual fact that some houses are blessed and others are cursed. The Bible says, "The Lord will curse the evil person's house, but he will bless the home of those who do right" (Proverbs 3:33).

There will always be girls who follow the crowd and hang out in the wrong places, but you don't have to be one of them. There is something called "guilt by association." People will generally assume that you are doing the same things that the people you hang with are doing. The Bible cautions, "Do not be fooled: 'Bad friends will ruin good habits'" (1 Corinthians 15:33).

Baby, I pray that you will decide to send a positive message to the boys who see you around. This is done by only letting them see you in respectable places. Let's go get a burger.

Think About It

I. Where do you like to hang out?_____

2. Do you feel that it is necessary to attend every school or social func-
   tion so that people can see you? Yes___ No___ Why? Or why not?

   Explain _____

3. Do you think that people are justified in feeling sorry for girls who
   hang out to attract attention from boys? Yes___ No___ Why? Or
   why not?

   Explain _____

4. Girls who hang out usually have an "I need to be seen mentality".
   How would you describe your mentality?

   _____

5. Do you feel that it is possible to hang with people and not adopt
   their thinking? Yes___ No___ Why? Or why not?

   Explain _____

6. What usually happens to nice girls who decide to play with games of
   temptation?_____

7. In your own opinion, are you mature enough to know what type of
   place is an inappropriate place for you to be in? Yes___ No___
   Why? Or why not?

   Explain _____

8. Write 1 Corinthians 15:33 here. _____

   _____.

9. Find and complete this sentence: People will generally assume that

   _____.

12 — No, Baby, Take Ten . . .

Here's the Deal . . .

You come to me and ask for five dollars to go to the mall with a young man. You go on to tell me that you will need to eat and pick up some personal items. I respond to you by saying:

BABY, DADDY doesn't ever want you to be in a situation where you don't have enough cash. When you are out with friends you should always have enough cash in your pocket to do several things. You should have at least enough cash to catch a bus, cab, or train home. At the very least, you should have enough money for necessary phone calls and always know a few people who you can contact.

Never place yourself in a position where you must solely depend on other people—especially young men! I am your daddy and until some young man marries you, you are my responsibility. Even though you are going to the mall with a young man, and I do like him, I don't want you to be dependent on him for anything! If you start officially dating and he chooses to spend money on you, that will be different. But even then you should be very careful to watch his attitude. If he starts acting like he owns you because he gave you something, that is an indication that he is not ready to date you.

When a young man spends money on a young woman, he always has a reason in mind. When the boy says that he doesn't, what he really means is that there may not be an immediate purpose for his generosity but a delayed one. You can take it from your dad that whenever a boy spends money on you, he will remember it. The Word of God has already proven the point that "borrowers are servants to lenders" (Proverbs 22:7). This is why I do not want a young man to feel like you owe him anything.

Money is extremely personal to men. To some men it is almost spiritual. It represents power, authority, freedom, and a secure future. You can't tell me that a young man will spend money on you without having an agenda. At the very least, he will do it because it makes him feel good. He also realizes that it may cause you to like him. When boys spend money on you, they will be very alert to observe your response. If a boy can detect that you are easily impressed when he purchases something for you, he will feel that you can be easily bought with money. If your response to the purchase is ho-hum, then he will keep wondering what makes you tick. Make sure that your response to a gift does not convey the image that you are extremely impressed. At the same time, you should thank him and be genuinely appreciative. I guess what I am trying to say is don't act like you have never had anything when you receive something from a young man.

Let me tell you what happens in the mind of a young man when you ask him for money and he gives it to you. His ego swells about 56 percent because men are turned on by their ability to provide. His self-esteem is boosted, and he begins to feel that he is important to you. Not only does he feel his giving is important, but he will not forget his investment. If he does have good intentions and is not trying to use you, then there is no problem. But if his intentions are not good, he may be scheming to have sex with you at some point. Taking money from him will only confuse him when he makes his move. He won't be happy when you tell him no.

I want you to make it a point with all of the boys that you meet to let them know that you have a dad who finances your needs. I want you to know that I will borrow or beg money and work four jobs if I have to before I let you borrow money from a young man. When you accept money from a young man, in his mind it drives a wedge between me and you. You see, money is personal! He will give you cash in an attempt to increase his level of influence in your life. If you are not careful, this will weaken our relationship because you have always received your money from me. Receiving money from another male will automatically cause your affections to shift; that would be premature—and I am not having it.

It is normal and natural for a young man to eventually take my place as your provider and protector. I will rejoice when that day comes and be glad for you. My only caution is—don't let it happen too soon and don't let it happen over a few dollars. The right time for this change to happen is after you are married.

After you have dated for a while and the young man consistently shows that he is willing to invest in you, after it is well established that the relationship is growing and maturing, then and only then can you consider freely taking his money or gifts without concern. Until then, take ten dollars and enjoy yourself at the mall.

Think About It

I. Do you take money when boys offer it to you? Yes___ No___ Why? Or why not?

Explain _____

2. Do you ask boys for money? Yes___ No___ Why? Or why not?

Explain _____

3. Has any boy ever acted like he owned you because he spent a few dollars on you? Yes___ No___

4. Do you keep some emergency cash on you at all times? Yes___ No___ Why? Or why not?

Explain _____

5. Name four people you could call in case you needed a ride home.

_____

_____

6. Find and complete this sentence: When a young man spends

_____.

7. If a young man detects that you are easily impressed with money, what will he think?

_____

8. What should your response be when you are given a gift?

_____

13 — Develop and Maintain Your Feminine Mystique

Here's the Deal . . .

Your mother and I just celebrated our nineteenth wedding anniversary. After all these years of marriage your mother still has something that keeps me coming back for more. That something is called the feminine mystique.

BABY, I WANT you to know something from the male perspective. The thing that makes a woman exciting is her mystique. The feminine mystique is a powerful endowment or gift that God has given to women. It is the one thing that men do not understand yet find very exciting. Men have written many love songs about this feminine characteristic, but no man has ever totally understood it.

Webster defines the word "mystique" as "a complex of somewhat mystical attitudes and feelings surrounding some person, institution, activity, etc." In other words, the female mystique is that thing about a woman that a man cannot figure out. As soon as the man feels like he has it down pat, the whole system, scheme, or strategy changes.

I can remember an occasion when my father was about

sixty-eight years old. He was frustrated with my mother because of something she did. In his frustration he looked at me and said: "Son, I just don't understand your mother!" At that point I realized how extremely challenging it is for a man and woman to understand each other.

The female mystique definitely makes living with a woman a challenge. But on the other hand, women who have no mystique about them soon become boring. They are 100 percent predictable all the time and cease to be a challenge very quickly. These women do not understand male/female differences, and as a result they fail to capitalize on those distinctions.

Let's look at a few qualities or components of the female mystique:

I. The ability of a woman to change her mind without any known reason. Any man who has lived with a woman knows that she changes her mind at will. One minute she wants to see this movie, and fifteen minutes later she wants to see that movie. One minute a woman wants Chinese food and the next minute she wants to go to a steak house.

Married men who are wise become accustomed to this and learn to be flexible in everything they do when spending time with their women. Having the ability to remain flexible helps keep the man alert so that he can be ready to deal with the decisions they must make as a couple. After having been married for a number of years, that man will do one of two things:

I. He will stop thinking through the available options because he knows that his wife has already figured it out; or,

2. He will aggressively challenge her when she changes her mind, and the two of them will have a very verbal and heated relationship.

2. The freedom to be moody. Everybody has changes in mood, but women seem to beat men in this area. Part of the reason is that a woman's mood changes are partly physical in nature. Some women seemingly go through four seasons in a month's time. Their behavior reflects the changes of the seasons just like spring, summer, fall, and winter. Most often they come as a result of the monthly cycle and the chemical changes that take place in the female body.

As a result of these internal changes taking place, women have a tendency to have mood swings. Most men are inclined to believe that women have mood swings not because of chemical changes in the body but because women are typically moodier than men.

Regardless of the true source of these mood swings, men must learn to deal with this aspect of the female mystique. Wise men learn to be sensitive to their woman's emotions and try to determine what type of mood she is in on a daily basis. As a matter of fact, the Bible commands men to be mindful of their woman's feelings: "You husbands should live with your wives in an understanding way, since they are weaker than you. But show them respect, because God gives them the same blessing he gives you—the grace that gives true life" (1 Peter 3:7).

3. The freedom to be weak when it is convenient. It is a known fact that women are some of the strongest creatures on planet Earth. Medical science has shown that women have bigger brains than men. Women can also endure more pain, which is particularly demonstrated through the trauma of childbirth—yet they are called the weaker sex. I believe they are considered the weaker sex because many females cannot lift as much physical weight as a man can. But in all other areas, women are superior to men. They live longer, have a better sense of smell and taste, and die of fewer diseases than men.

In spite of all this, there are times when they appear to be very weak. Sometimes women experience weakness because something genuinely frightens them. At other times, women use their high intellect to appear weak as a means to get what they want. All wise women know how to capitalize on this aspect of the female mystique.

4. The ability to totally miss the point and make it seem insignificant. Nobody knows everything. When a man does not know something, he is ignorant or dumb in that area. When a woman does not know something, she may call the thing that she does not know "stupid." For example, when a woman's car won't start, she says: "The stupid car won't start." The man explains that the battery is dead. She says: "That's not the point; the point is that the car won't start." The man says: "We can get a new battery and everything will be all right." She still says: "The stupid car won't start." Wise men understand this and will hurry up and buy a new battery and put it in the car before she decides that she wants to buy a new car.

My daughter, please note that the mystique is in full force when you first meet a guy. You must be wise and make the mystique work for you. Let's consider how to maintain your mystique:

1. Disclose yourself to your man slowly. Think about this point. When a guy meets you, he wants to know all that he can know about you as fast as he can. Well, this is good for him and bad for you. Young men do not understand the female mystique, and their ignorance of it is a clear advantage for the young lady. One of the things that makes young girls boring to older men is that older men have figured out the mystique of a young girl and they no longer respect it.

Men respect the mystique of thinking women their age because these women have continued to develop their mystique over the years and have become experts at keeping a man wondering what she is going to do next. Baby, you can quickly become boring to a guy when you tell him everything that he wants to know too soon. Your mother still keeps me guessing, and the challenge keeps me coming back for more.

2. Always keep a part of you to yourself. Your mystique will develop in sophistication when there is a part of you that nobody knows. I think the best example of this would be your relationship with God. The intimate details of your personal relationship with the Lord are unknown to anyone else. As that relationship grows it provides a source of strength that others will visibly see and appreciate but not fully understand. The apostle Paul understood the value of having a spirit that is built up and established in God, and so he prayed for the church: "I ask the Father in his great glory to give you the power to be strong inwardly through his Spirit" (Ephesians 3:16). If you keep this prayer in mind, you will benefit from the internal strength that you will receive from God.

3. Be a lifelong learner. Many women make the mistake of settling down once they get their man. This is a mistake. Actually, you should really work to learn more once you have a mate because your life is now more complicated than it was when you were alone. Learn more about relationships, how to invest your money, how to serve God better, and how to serve others better. In other words, prepare for your future so that it does not catch you unprepared.

A woman who continues to learn, grow, and develop after she is in a relationship will have a greater chance of keeping the man interested in being with her. Remember, I am talking about a thinking man, not a bum.

4. Become knowledgeable in the areas where your man has knowledge. If he is into sports, read up on his favorite teams and impress him with your knowledge. This will cause him to be on his toes and pay attention when you are speaking.

It is a very disappointing thing when a woman loses her mystique. That woman becomes dull, predictable, conquered, and will quickly become a disposable liability. I will say it again, my wife of nineteen years is just as challenging today as she was when I first met her. It's because she maintains her mystique.

Think About It

1. What are you doing right now to improve yourself?

   _____

2. Define the female mystique in your own words. _____

   _____

3. Do you feel that you have a female mystique about you? Yes___ No___ Were you aware of it before you read this chapter? Yes___ No___

4. When is the female mystique in full force? _____

   _____

5. Do young guys usually understand the female mystique? Yes___ No___ Why? Or why not?

   Explain _____

6. Why did the author say thinking men enjoy the female mystique?

   _____

7. What happens when a girl loses her mystique?

   _____

8. When you first meet a guy, do you tell him everything the first time you really talk? Yes___ No___

9. How do you feel a relationship with God affects your female mystique? _____

   _____

10. Are you a lifelong learner? Yes___ No___ Why? Or why not?

    Explain _____

11. I have tried to explain the feminine mystique from the male perspective. I am sure that there are many men and women who will disagree with my views. Do you think that I am accurate___, inaccurate___, in between___, other___?

    Explain _____

    _____

14)—You and Your Momma

Here's the Deal . . .

We attend a school basketball game together. The mother of one of the girls on the team is acting loud and rowdy in the stands. This mom really put on a show. You inform me that the daughter acts the same way. This is the conversation that follows.

BABY, YOUR mother and I have worked hard to raise you in a godly manner. We have sought to create a home environment where you could observe and learn how a man and woman should relate to each other in a healthy way. I know that we have not been perfect parents, but I do feel that you have been blessed with a good home.

As you develop into a mature woman, you will have to make some decisions about the type of mother you want to be. Don't just grow up and turn out any old way. Decide what you want to be like and then work toward that goal. You have the power to control and direct many aspects of your future life.

Most girls end up being a lot like their mothers simply because they never gave any thought to what they want to be like. As a result, they unconsciously end up being just like Mom. This can be good or it can be bad. In your case, you have a wonderful mother who is in my eyes a "31:10." The Bible tells us, "It is hard to find a good wife, because she is worth more than rubies" (Proverbs 31:10). If you do as well as your mother, you will be blessed, and your future husband will be blessed as well.

What I want you to think about are those areas where you want to improve upon how your mom does things. Give some thought to those areas and consider what you would change in your life. For example:

1. Her attitude about men, including her ability to understand and relate to men
2. The amount of time she spends cooking and cleaning the house
3. The amount of time she spends working outside the home
4. The way she disciplines you
5. Her personal grooming
6. The way she handles money

These are just a few of the areas where you should decide how you want to conduct yourself. It will take some very intentional prayers on your part when you are ready to make sound decisions about which behaviors to modify and which ones to eliminate altogether. Have you talked with your mother about the things you need to do to improve your life? Have you asked her to share her mistakes with you to help you avoid them? After all, we are to learn from the mistakes of the previous generation so that we don't repeat them.

I know of girls who have said that they need to do better than their moms in some ways, primarily in the area of relationships with men. Too many mothers have not set a good example for their daughters. In some cases, these moms were innocent victims of abusive men. There are women who have allowed their men to abuse them while their daughters observed the tragedy of it all. Other women have had relationships with a string of various men while their daughters watched.

I was visiting a middle school the other day, and a young mother was standing in the hallway with her hand on her hip cursing at the dean. She was being really loud, and her behavior was very wrong. I felt sorry for her because she was definitely not demonstrating intelligence. The principal told me that the daughter had just cursed at the dean the day before. Like mother, like daughter. A girl modeling her mom's behavior can either be a good thing or it can be bad. In this case it was really bad.

There is no such thing as a perfect parent. The fact is that most children end up adopting both good and bad traits from their parents. Having lived with them all of their lives, most kids act a lot like their parents, even though they say they would never do some of the things they witnessed their parents doing. The goal is to learn to embrace the good while eliminating the bad. As children grow older it becomes their job to do an ongoing self-evaluation to see what bad habits they need to get rid of and then get busy working on them with God's help. This is called taking on the responsibility of becoming an adult.

As the saying goes, "It takes a whole village to raise a child." The point that needs to be understood is that parents don't know everything. It may be necessary for some young people to go to another adult to learn things that their own parents may not know or be able to teach them. For example, my dad knew nothing about music, so I learned about music from another adult. My parents could not help me with advanced math, so I learned that subject from another adult.

Baby, it is wise to learn the things we need to know from others when our parents are not able to teach us. Whether you are getting help from your own momma or from someone else, the key is to get all the understanding you can to improve yourself. The Bible has everything good to say about having wisdom. So always remember this: "Listen to advice and accept correction, and in the end you will be wise" (Proverbs 19:20).

Think About It

1. Do you have any bad habits? Yes___ No___ What are they?

_____

_____

2. What good habits does your mother have that you want to develop?

_____

3. What habit does your mother have that you do not want to develop?

_____

4. What is a "31:10"?

_____

5. Did you know that you can decide how you want to act? Yes___
No___

6. Do you think that your mother will share her mistakes with you and show you how to avoid them? Yes___ No___

Why? Or why not? Explain _____

_____

7. How would you like to be described by your own children: weak ___, wicked ___, worrisome ___, or wonderful ___?

Part 4

Advice from Dad

15)—Don't Call Boys on the Phone— Let Them Call You!

Here's the Deal . . .

Dad notices that you are spending a lot of time talking to boys on the phone. Dad also notices that you are talking, but the phone does not ring. So I assume that you are doing most of the calling.

BABY, DADDY knows that you called a young man the other day. I want you to know that Daddy doesn't want you to call boys on the phone. My attitude is that you are the prize, and if boys cannot at least make an effort to get in touch with you, then you should not call them.

There are several reasons why you should not call boys:

1. It makes their heads swell, and they begin to think that you cannot live without them.

2. You become less of a challenge when you go after them.

3. You become less interesting to them.

4. They begin to feel like you are chasing them.

The general rule is: As a girl, you should not initiate the conversation. To initiate something is to start something, and no relationship should be initiated by the girl! If you initiate the relationship, the boy will get tired of you more quickly than if he starts the relationship by pursuing you. A boy can initiate a relationship and work on keeping it together. A girl can initiate a relationship and get the boy, but it is less likely that she can keep the relationship together.

With most breakups, it is the guy who leaves. When marriages fail, it is usually the man who leaves. The man is called the "husband." If we divide that word, you will see what I mean. He is the hus-band. He is the band that holds the family together. A man who tries hard has better success at keeping a woman than a woman has at keeping a man. The reason is that when a young man starts the relationship, he is motivated by love to keep it together. When the girl starts the relationship, the guy may or may not even love her. He may grow to like her a good deal or eventually love her, but it is not the same as if he had started the relationship.

A very wise man in the Bible known as Boaz recognized the importance of a girl not pursuing a guy. When he addressed his future wife, Ruth, he said to her, "The Lord bless you, my daughter . . . You didn't look for a young man to marry, either rich or poor. Now, my daughter, don't be afraid. I will do everything you ask, because all the people in our town know you are a good woman" (Ruth 3:10–11). This young lady was rewarded for strong sense of character; she did not compromise her desire to do right in the right way.

I realize that girls today call on boys and ask them if they are interested in a relationship. But that is not the best way to do it. When Daddy tells you these things, I know you get tired of listening. However, I want you to remember one thing: Times have changed, but human nature has not.

Let me explain further what happens when you call a boy:

1. It makes their heads swell, and they begin to think that you cannot live without them. It is the ego factor that I believe is worse today than it has ever been. Young boys have huge egos and very rarely have they learned how to control them. I don't care if the young man is tall, short, smart, dumb, broke, or rich; the young man has an ego.

When you call the boy, it makes his ego feel good. The only problem with his ego feeling good is that when this happens, he usually thinks of you serving him instead of him serving you.

If you ever have a relationship where you are seen as the neediest person in the relationship, you are in for a life of servitude. The man will feel like you can't live without him and will expect you to serve him forever. You will have a "honey do" life: "Honey, do this; honey, do that."

I also said that when you constantly call boys on the phone something else happens:

2. You become less of a challenge when you go after them.

In a healthy relationship it is a necessary step for boys to woo and win their girlfriends. If you just fall in the boy's lap, then he did not work for the relationship. Thus, he will not value it. "Easy come, easy go" will be his attitude. Please remember that I am a man and the son of a man, and I know what I am talking about.

I can recall the stories my father told me about his dating experiences. I assure you, the same principles that applied in the 1930s still apply today. When I decided to get married, there were three girls whom I knew well enough to ask to marry me. One of them was pretty but silly, and I did not ask her because of that. Another one told me that she would cook, clean, and do whatever I needed if I would marry her. I did not marry her because she was a little too anxious and eager.

Then there was your mother. She showed no interest in me at all. But she allowed me to talk to her, spend time with her, and eventually allowed me to touch her. As a man, I enjoyed the challenge. If she had fallen all over me, I probably would have looked for someone less needy.

3. You become less interesting to them.

Once you are no longer a challenge, you are no longer interesting. I was watching a basketball game the other day when one team was ahead thirty-five points. The game was no longer a challenge for the winning team, and they began to play around and goof off.

4. They begin to feel like you are chasing them.

This is the most important reason that you should not call the boy all the time. I can't think of anything worse than a girl who chases a boy. As your dad, it would be very humiliating to think that you are chasing boys. It makes you look like you are starved for attention and not receiving love and hugs at home.

Baby, it is normal to sometimes feel lonely or unloved. But the fact of the matter is, you are loved very much. Come and talk to me if you need to, but please don't dial a boy's number unless he is dialing yours much more often than you are dialing his.

Think About It

I. Do you call boys on the phone? Yes___ No___ If so, how often?

_____

2. How do your parents feel about you calling boys on the phone?

_____

3. Do you agree with the author when it comes to girls initiating relationships with boys? Yes___ No___

4. Have you ever seen a marriage or a dating relationship where it looked like the man did not want the woman? Yes___ No___

5. Go back to the beginning of the chapter and read the four reasons why you should not make a habit of calling boys.

6. Do you view yourself as a cheap prize or a very valuable prize that some wise boy will claim someday?

_____

7. The author talked about the women he had to choose from before he got married. If you were one of them, which one would you have been?

_____

8. The author is not saying that girls should never call boys. What do you understand him to say in this chapter?

_____

9. After reading this chapter, what is your attitude about calling boys?

_____

16)—Dating? Not Until You're 16!

Here's the Deal . . .

A seventeen-year-old young man has asked you to go on a date. I know that he is a good boy who has his license and drives his mother's car. You are currently fifteen years old. Here is what Dad has to say to you.

BABY, YOUR daddy's job has two aspects to it. The first one is to provide for you. Ever since you were born, it has been a passion of mine to see that you have a place to live, food to eat, clothes to wear, lots of hugs, and some doll babies to play with. The second aspect of my job is to protect you. At this point in your life, you can't understand why your dad will not let you go on a date with this young man. I really don't expect you to totally understand, but you should find it interesting that your mother agrees with me. If your mother was saying, "Let her go to the party," then it would be a different thing, but she agrees with me.

You are a very mature young lady for your age, but that has nothing to do with the fact that you should not go on this date. You are completely trusted by your parents, but in spite of that fact, we are still not going to let you go on this date.

There is a very good reason for my passion about this. Listen to this fact: The earlier in life young people begin to date, the earlier they become sexually active. I know that you are not planning to marry this guy, but by being with him you put yourself on the firing line. I know that everybody is doing it, but I couldn't care less about what others are doing. Dating is not a mandatory activity.

People say that you should date for the following reasons:

I. Fun

It can be fun going places and doing things with boys. But you can have fun doing activities with boys without going on a "date" with them. The word *date* speaks of exclusivity and intimacy; it would open the door to other things that are not even a possibility for you right now. Your father is all for fun. I believe that it is necessary to have fun to be healthy. However, there are other options for having fun with boys than going on a date with them.

2. Friendship

You can have friends without dating them or being romantically involved. My definition of dating is to spend time with a person with the intent of getting to know them well enough to decide if you want to get serious about them! Dating is a relationship that could lead to intimacy. Everybody marries someone whom they dated. So, in my opinion, dating is not an innocent and unintentional activity, but a serious encounter with a young man that could have permanent results. Remember, the person you date may become your mate, so be careful about dating people you would not want to marry.

3. To Learn about the Opposite Sex

I want to state that you can learn about the male sex without dating numerous men. Many young girls today have believed the lie that they are supposed to have "experience" before they get married. This is just the opposite of what God says. God says that you are to go to your marriage bed with no sexual experience.

It has been said that experience is the best teacher. Well, experience is a great teacher, but it can cause you to learn about something the hard way. That's why it is best to learn about difficult things in life from the experience of others as much as possible. What I am saying to you is, let other people's pain be your gain. Learn from it. With experience comes problems and pain that usually outweigh the pleasure. When experience is gained prematurely or while the girl is too young to handle it, the situation can lead to parking, petting, and pregnancy. As your dad, it is my job to protect you from experiencing certain things prematurely.

Be sure not to get your advice from TV or other ungodly sources. Many adults are sex crazed, and they want others to place sexual pleasure as the priority in their lives as well. I want you to know that if you wait on the Lord, He will give you just what you need in a mate. If you run ahead and look for someone on your own, you will most likely be disappointed. The way to avoid disappointment in life is to do what Jesus said for us to do: "Seek first God's kingdom and what God wants. Then all your other needs will be met as well" (Matthew 6:33).

Baby, Daddy wants you to have a well-rounded life. An obsession with going out on a date may show that there are some questions that need to be asked and issues that you need to deal with, such as:

1. Do you have a healthy love for yourself? A twenty-six-year-old fatherless lady once stated: "I tried to find my identity in my boyfriend who became my husband. He taught me all the wrong things."

2. Are you allowing peer pressure to push you? I challenge you to be an individual and don't follow the crowd.

3. Are you committed to staying a virgin until you marry? Just because you have sexual urges does not mean that it is time to have sex. Don't date with a secret agenda in the back of your mind, thinking that you are ready to lose your virginity.

4. Have you forgotten that a crush is a temporary feeling that will soon go away? Crushes quickly crumble. Just compare the boys you like now to the ones you liked one or two years ago.

5. Is Jesus still your number one man with Dad being number two and your date a distant third? Remember that you are actually married to Jesus until a man puts a ring on your finger.

BABY, I AM going to hush now, but I want you to remember that dating is serious business, too serious to enter into without counsel from the wise adults in your life. I am here if you need to talk. I love you, and I'm committed to taking care of you.

Love, Dad

Think About It

I. Are you dating someone right now? Yes___ No___ Why? Or why not?

Explain _____

2. Have you thought about why you want to date? Yes___ No___

3. If you answered yes to the previous question, tell why.

_____

4. What is the greatest source of pressure you feel when it comes to dating? Check one: Peer pressure ___
You feel lonely. ___
It makes you feel pretty. ___
Because you just want to ___
It satisfies you. ___
You need to be around a young man. ___

5. How well do you feel that you know boys?
Very well ___
Well ___
Somewhat well ___
Not well ___

6. What has been your main source of information about boys?

_____

7. Would you feel comfortable talking to your dad about boys? Yes___ No___

Explain _____

8. If your dad is not around, what other man would you talk to about boys? _____

9. Find and complete this sentence. The earlier young people begin to date, _____.

17)—The Importance of Your First Date

Here's the Deal . . .

You are fifteen years old. One afternoon over lunch you hinted around that you thought you were ready to start dating. I think you were just trying to feel me out to see what my reaction would be. But as your concerned dad, this is what I had to share with you.

WHEN A BOY starts to like you, you develop a paradigm (a way of thinking) about relationships and boys based on how he treats you. For example, the way that he talks to you, touches you, and responds to your conversation will be recorded in your mind. The way that you interact and respond to other young men in the future will be influenced by the manner in which your first boyfriend treats you. This is why it is so very important to be careful to choose who your first date will be.

When I ask you about your boyfriends, I want you to understand that it is very important that you are honest with me. I need to provide you with guidance during these early years of your dating experience. Everybody has a first date, and most adults will look back at their first date and shake their heads in amusement as they remember how funny it was. You will probably do the same thing when you get older.

As your father, it is my responsibility to present you to your husband on your wedding day. When I present you, I don't want you to have a lot of bad memories from the numerous guys who dated you before marriage. Statistics clearly show that if young people begin to date early, they also have sex earlier. With this in mind, here are a few things I want you to consider:

The appropriate age to date. Baby, Daddy wants you to know that girls should not date before they are sixteen years old. As a matter of fact, don't even come to me and ask if you can date until you are at least sixteen. In fact, I need to know that you are mature enough and ready to date at sixteen; otherwise, you may not be able to date even then. Dad knows what he is doing. I remember what happened to girls who started dating when they were very young. The maturity needed to make good decisions is not there for most girls before they are sixteen.

So, baby, in this house you will need to wait until you are at least sixteen and maybe not even then. If you need to get out of the house, we can go bowling or something, but don't expect a young man in a car to come to this house and pick you up to take you out somewhere.

Boyfriends represent a gradual separation from parents. The maturing of children can be a powerful and painful, but positive, experience in the life of a parent. I want to keep reminding you throughout these talks that you should be patient with your parents because taking care of children is a huge responsibility, and we have never been this old before.

Parents' pain. As I look at you turning into a young lady, I continue to realize that in a few years I will no longer be the number one man in your life. This will break my heart, but that is life and I will survive. For dads, it is very hard and painful to see their daughters grow up.

Just like you are going through a transition, your dad is going through a transition, and you can help my pain by exhibiting wisdom as you relate to boys. Your dad will make it through his transition, but you can ease the pain if we communicate and you allow me to participate.

Parents' pleasure. The pain of losing you to a young man is soon replaced with the pleasure of seeing you functioning as a responsible young adult in society. It brings great joy to a dad's heart to know that his daughter is intelligent and acts accordingly. As I have said to you since you were a little girl, Daddy only gets angry with you when you don't think! So keep thinking and making good decisions, and your dad will be happy.

At times, I may act like I want you to stay a little girl forever, but the fact of the matter is I will be very excited when you become a stable adult. It is just that we must be very careful during this time of transition when you feel that you are almost grown up and you are in the process of developing into a beautiful young woman. There are areas of your strength and training that have not yet been tested. I know that if you fail in some of these areas, the results can be devastating. That is why I am so concerned for you, because following my guidance can help you avoid experiencing some painful issues.

Do you remember when you first got your student learner's permit? You made a few mistakes initially when you began to drive on the road. Mistakes like failing to look left before entering the intersection or failing to look over your right shoulder in the blind spot before you changed lanes. Such oversights could have been devastating, but I was there to warn you when you made those errors.

Now, my options are to either sit in the backseat of the car on all of your dates or to allow you to go out with a boy and trust that you will practice what I have shared with you.

Kissing on your first date. Let's talk about it. Baby, never kiss an old nasty-mouthed boy on your first date. You don't know him well enough to kiss. You don't even know if he brushes his teeth or if he just covers up his bad breath with breath mints. He may have had snails for dinner or something like that. Kissing is a very intimate activity that should be reserved for serious, not casual, relationships. I have studied the Bible, and I can't find where people kissed much. The most famous kiss in the Bible is when Judas kissed Jesus as a sign that He was the One to be arrested.

The more I think about it, kissing is something that should be reserved for much later in a relationship. Be satisfied with holding his hand for quite a while before you kiss him. Physical touch should not be on your mind on the first date or in the early stages of a relationship.

Think About It

I. Are you in a rush to go on a first date? Yes___ No___ Why? Or why not?
Explain _____

2. Do you realize that the more you are alone with a guy, the greater your chances are of having sex prematurely? Yes___ No___

3. Do you feel that the author is old-fashioned or overprotective of his daughter? Yes___ No___ Why? Or why not?

Explain _____

4. Some girls say that all guys are dogs. Although this is not true, why do you feel that they would say that?

_____

5. Find and complete this sentence: Boyfriends represent a gradual

_____.

6. When you begin to date, who goes through a transition?

_____

7. How do you feel about kissing on your first date?_____

_____

8. Do you feel like your parents want you to stay young forever? Yes___ No___

9. How is going on your first date different from having your student learner's permit?_____

IO. How old do you feel you should be on your first date?

_____

18—Tell Your Friend Not to Blow in Front of My House!

Here's the Deal...

It is a Saturday afternoon and you have just turned seventeen. You asked to go bowling with a young man. He pulls up in front of the house in his mom's car and blows the horn like he is half deaf. This is what Dad has to say to you before you go out the door.

BABY, DO YOU want me to go outside and talk to that young man? He should know better than to blow his horn in front of a girl's house like that. I am disappointed in him. I thought he had more class than that. How long have you been seeing him? You answer: "Three weeks." Dad replies: "It's only been three weeks, and the brother will not come to the door and ask you out? Something is wrong here."

I go on to instruct you to tell him not to blow in front of my house. I have some fundamental concerns when a young man will not get out of the car to pick up a girl whom he is supposed to be excited about going out with. It is not OK for a boy to blow his horn in front of a young lady's house. This bothers me and I will tell you why.

I. He is supposed to be excited that you are going out with him. If you just needed a ride, I could have taken you, but when a boy picks you up, it means that he sees something special in you. If he sees something special in you, then he should be able to get out of the car, come to the door, and ask for you.

2. If he is not excited about going out with you, then you should not get in the car with him. You see, baby, you never go out with a guy who is just tolerating you or simply going out with you instead of doing something else like watching TV. It is dangerous to be with a boy who has minimal or no interest in you. What if you are out somewhere and there is a need for him to protect you? Would he be willing in some way to risk himself on your behalf? If he is with you just to kill time, you would be better off if you had gone with your brother, father, or someone who would look after you.

This young man's behavior gives me some concerns about him. Anyone who would pull up in front of the house and blow like he just did makes me wonder what he is up to. Don't get me wrong; maybe no one ever told the boy how it affects a father to hear someone blow the horn for his daughter. I want you to tell him, or I will talk with him because what he just did was not wise. Let me remind you that it is my job to protect you, and I am going to watch everything that your boyfriend does. It is my responsibility to examine him and look for cracks in his armor. I want to see what he is made of.

Think about this: when a relationship begins, the guy usually dates the girl and tries to win her heart. This can be a great time for the girl, because if she will ever get flowers and candy, it will be now. If someone ever opens doors for her, it will be now. This period of courting is a time that a young lady will appreciate the most because the guy will treat her so well.

My point is that the brother must prove himself now by coming to the door to greet you. He must be motivated enough to get out of the car, walk to the door, and say something intelligent like: "Are you ready to go?" If he cannot treat you with common courtesy at this point, how do you think he is going to treat you later? I am talking about a matter of showing you the proper respect.

I have been married for nineteen years, and I still don't sit in front of the house and blast the horn when I am waiting for my wife. There is something degrading about doing that, and she will not go for it. I don't suggest that you go for it either.

As your father, I never want to see you jump when a boy snaps his fingers, claps his hands, opens his wallet, or blows his horn. When you are seen running to the car when a horn blows, it is a sign that the brother has too much control over your mind and you are not exercising restraint.

It is the nature of a young man to get away with as much as his girl will allow. I married a woman who insists that I treat her with dignity and respect all the time, and she does not play. So it's simple. I treat her with love and respect, and she is the sweetest woman you have ever seen. If I were to lower the standard and treat her like less than the lady she is, there would be trouble in the camp.

Please realize that I am thinking long range. I am considering the patterns that you are setting in the relationship now that will affect you years later. Many girls ruin their relationships before they start by giving their guys too much freedom in the way they are treated. I have known women to allow their men to do almost anything while they were dating, and when they got married they thought the man would suddenly begin to treat them with dignity. It just doesn't happen that way.

Patterns are set early in the relationship, and it will take much more effort to change behavior from negative to positive than it will to establish certain expectations and behaviors in the beginning of the relationship.

Let me say that I would not act like this if there were a car full of young people out there in the driveway. They would be talking and having fun. It would not be as intimate as a young man picking you up by himself. If the brother is going to come alone, then he has to show all the expected courtesies.

Now, go on out to the car. We've made him wait a few minutes. I suggest that you school him while you are with him today. Let him know what your expectations are, and remember that you always have my permission to break up with him. Take my cell phone and call me if you are not happy with his response.

Think About It

1. Do you feel that Dad was too hard on the young man who blew the horn? Yes___ No___

Explain _____

2. Is it reasonable today to expect boys to open doors and treat girls with respect? Yes___ No___

Explain _____

3. Do you feel that it is important for a guy to be courteous in the beginning of the relationship? Yes___ No___ Why? Or why not?

Explain _____

4. There is a lot of sexual equality being preached these days. Do you feel that a girl is weaker when she expects a guy to treat her with respect? Yes___ No___

5. Was Dad being reasonable or too picky?_____

_____

6. Dad made the point that if the boy won't treat you special now, what can you expect later. How do you feel about this? _____

_____

7. Do you feel that it is OK for the girl who drives to blow for the boy she is picking up? Yes___ No___

8. What was Dad saying when he gave his daughter his cell phone?

_____

9. What can you do in the beginning of your relationship that will help your boyfriend treat you properly throughout your relationship?

_____

19)—Don't Stay on the Hook Too Long

Here's the Deal . . .

I ask you about the young man who has been showing an interest in you. I mention that I hadn't heard you talking about him in a while. You respond with the statement that he only calls every now and then. This is my advice to you.

BABY, DADDY wants you to know that young men enjoy the company of pretty young girls. They just like to be around you. A young man will do things to increase his potential of finding the right young lady. In many cases this man will have more than one girl, or he will keep one hanging on while he tries to make up his mind. There are a million excuses that he will use to indicate why he will not commit himself to you or anyone else. Excuses like: "I'm not ready yet; I need to find myself; I need to get my finances together; I don't want to rush," etc.

I compare this whole situation to fishing. Guys basically will "fish" in a school of girls in an attempt to find the right one. They will cast their lure into the water in search of "the big one." The many "fish" who are out there will sample the bait, and if they like the bait, they will bite. At this point, the hook is in a girl's mouth and the young man is holding the pole to which the hook is attached.

When a fisherman hooks a fish, he has several goals. The first goal is to make sure that the hook is firmly stuck in the fish's mouth. This is called "setting the hook." Once the fish is firmly hooked, it can then be safely reeled in. Oftentimes, guys will go to great lengths to make sure that they have invested enough time and energy into getting a girl interested. This is the setting of the hook. Once the hook is set, the fish will not get away, and the fisherman knows that it is just a matter of time until he reels the fish in. What happens next is very important. After the fisherman hooks the fish, he reels it in, removes it from the hook, and takes it home.

I remember on one occasion, I caught a big catfish. I was happy to have hooked that fish. The fish was hooked securely on my line, and I was able to let him swim around in the water for a long time before I finally reeled him in. That was fun! But the right thing for a fisherman to do after he gets the fish to shore is to take the fish off of the hook and either take it home to enjoy or release the fish to regain its freedom and continue living.

But, in many cases, men will not do that. What they will do is reel the fish in to the shore and then press the release button on their reel and allow the fish to swim out into the water again. The fisherman will then have the joy of reeling the same fish in again like I did with the catfish. This is done over and over until the fish is exhausted.

If a young man really wants to have a serious relationship, he will hook you, reel you in, take you off the hook, and begin working to make you a vital part of his life. If he is simply enjoying the thrill of hooking a big, beautiful fish, he will just keep you on the line and play with you for a while like the fisherman who is fishing for the enjoyment of the sport.

Baby, never let a young man play with you for a long time before he reels you in. In other words, don't be a boy's plaything while he tries to decide if he wants to grow up and make a commitment to you. If a young man procrastinates when it comes to proceeding with the relationship, there may be several reasons:

I. He may be undecided. If this is the case, he won't keep playing; he will eventually make a decision. If he decides that you are not the one, say: "Praise the Lord!" and wait on God to bring you someone better.

2. He may be cautious. If this is the case, he will not be hot and cold but consistent in his interactions with you. There is a difference between when you're being played and when a young man needs you to be patient with him.

3. He may be a player. Players can be identified because of the lies they tell, their lack of commitment, their inability to sacrifice for others, and they are known for their bad reputation. This type of individual should be avoided like the plague.

Some guys will hook young women with the hook of love and bring them almost to a commitment of marriage. Then they will start some argument that will cause a breakup. This is the same process as letting the girl swim out into the middle of the lake again. So many young women will allow a guy to treat them any old way while he tries to make up his mind.

If you respond to his initial interest in you, don't wait forever for him to decide that he wants to take the relationship to the next level. If the young man is serious about you, he will first want to be an acquaintance, then a friend, then a close friend, and finally an intimate friend. This is the way to build a foundation for a solid marriage.

Baby, check this out: Daddy doesn't ever want you to be a boy's toy. I won't be able to handle that, no matter how old I get. Never forget this:

IF YOU DON'T HAVE A COMMITMENT, YOU DON'T HAVE ANYTHING.

Now, I am not saying that you shouldn't talk to guys and have extended relationships. What I am saying is that you can't allow yourself to stay on the line forever. There should always be some progression in the relationship that would be proof that the young man has future plans that include you.

It is very important to be able to identify when a guy is just keeping you on the line. However, you must be able to find out without nagging him, and it takes wisdom and discernment to do this. If you want to know how to recognize when you have been on the line too long, look for these signs:

- ❀ He is not responsive to your basic requests like calling you, speaking nicely to you, and showing you basic courtesies and kindnesses.
- ❀ He is only motivated by your threats of separation.
- ❀ As time passes, his commitment to you does not increase.

Always have a wise woman like your mother to advise you. When you do look for advice from others, it would be best for you to talk with a woman who has had good relationships with men and is not angry with men in general.

By the way, I never told you what I did with the fish that stayed on the line. I played with it until the fish was exhausted. Actually, the fish became so tired that it just rose to the top of the water and floated on its side. When you let a man keep you on the line too long, he will eventually wear you down, and you will be too tired to think clearly. He could end up outsmarting you, and you could possibly get hurt! Baby, listen to your old dad and don't stay on the line too long.

Just like a fish can spit out a hook before it becomes firmly set in its mouth, a young lady can reject a guy and cause minimal damage if she does it early in the relationship. You will definitely want to reject hooks when you can tell that the guy holding the pole is a low-quality prospect. For your own protection, I don't want to see you stay on the line too long.

Think About It

1. Is it hard for you to get a hint that the boy does not like you, like when a boy tells you he can't talk to you right now because he needs to watch his clothes dry? Yes___ No___

2. Commitment is a key indication of interest. Do you have any problem dropping a boy when he doesn't give you a commitment? Yes___ No___

3. The author gives three categories of young men who procrastinate as it relates to commitment. Can you think of any additional reasons?

   _____

4. Find and complete this sentence:

   If you don't _____.

5. If you stay on the line too long you will eventually become _____ _____, and what will happen then? _____

   _____

6. It is easier to stop a relationship if you do it _____

   _____

7. The author gives three signs that may indicate that the boy is keeping you on the line. Write them here:

   _____

   _____

   _____

8. According to Dad, what type of woman should you seek advice from?

   _____

   _____

20)—Heartbreak Is Inevitable

BABY, I WANT you to know that everybody gets a broken heart at some point in life. I wish that there was some way that I could save you from the pain, but it is not possible to live and not suffer a broken heart. A heartbreak can come in many areas of life, not just relationships. Even though everybody experiences it, there are some things that can be done to keep the heartbreak caused by young men to a minimum. But through it all you can hold on to God's promise that "he heals the brokenhearted and bandages their wounds" (Psalm 147:3).

1. Screen your dates carefully. Some girls fall in love too quickly. Not only do they fall in love too quickly, but they fall in love with people they like and not necessarily people who like them in the same way. You help your odds for a successful relationship when the person you date likes you more than you like him. Too often young people just end up going out together with no clear understanding of why they are together. They are not aware of the rules that will guide their relationships. This is common when you are young, but it is also a common mistake for older people. Problems result in a relationship when you don't know why you started going out together in the first place.

You are asking for trouble when you get into a relationship with a young man and you cannot identify and communicate some definite reasons for why you want to be involved with him.

2. Seek to have a limited number of relationships. It is simply a lie that you must be dating somebody to be considered a normal person. Countless young girls have become involved in relationships only because their friends were involved in relationships. It is really not a smart thing to do. This is due to peer pressure, and it comes from the lie that you will not be "normal" if you don't have a steady date by a certain age.

In ancient times, people did not date; they just got married when they were old enough to be married. Usually their parents picked their husband/wife for them. Yes, this is ancient history, but it prevented excessive heartbreaks. Besides, who said that you have to date thirty-six boys before you get married anyway? The fewer people you date, the less psychological damage you will suffer. Our society promotes dating because it promotes premarital sex, which the Bible calls fornication. You may have even heard stories about people who have experienced the pain that has resulted from engaging in sex before marriage.

3. Make sure that your self-esteem is intact. People often date for the wrong reasons. They date someone so that they can feel better about themselves. But the truth is, no other person can help you feel good about yourself for the rest of your life. Other people can only help you feel better about yourself for a little while. You have to know for yourself that you are important and that you matter to God.

God assures us that He loves us unconditionally when we belong to Him: "And from far away the Lord appeared to his people and said, 'I love you people with a love that will last forever. That is why I have continued showing you kindness'" (Jeremiah 31:3). When you can really see that you mean more than this whole world to God, your parents, and close friends, then you will begin to realize how are valuable you are.

As you read the following Scripture, put your name in the blank space. Do this as many times as needed to give you an idea of how much God loves you.

> "God loved _____ so much that he gave his one and only Son so that [if] _____ believes in him _____ may not be lost, but have eternal life" (John 3:16).

4. Focus on your personal goals. Every young woman should prepare for her future as if she is going to be single. By this I mean that you should have career plans that can sustain you as a single woman. Don't put all your eggs in the basket of meeting "Prince Charming" and someday getting married. Work on your grade point average so that you can get into college. Establish yourself in such a manner that if a young man does or does not come along, you are prepared either way. The bottom line is that you can be flexible without neglecting to plan for your future.

Decide now to get a master's or Ph.D. degree in an area of your interest so that when you complete your bachelor's degree, you will go back and get some additional degrees. It was my idea that my wife should earn her doctorate degree. The reason I wanted her to have one was so she could take care of herself if something happened to me. Plan your goals, and by all means ask for assistance if you need help in establishing them.

5. In the middle of all heartbreaks, claim Romans 8:28. "We know that in everything God works for the good of those who love him. They are the people he called, because that was his plan." As I look back on my life, I praise God for my heartbreaks because they were used to take me to higher levels of understanding.

I can remember when my best girlfriend broke up with me in college. I literally thought that I would die. I thought I would never breathe again or eat another burger—but those things didn't happen. I lived and found another relationship better than the one I had. When you suffer heartbreak, remember that God has promised to make it turn out for good if you love and belong to Him.

6. Embrace I Corinthians 7:34. "A woman who is not married or a girl who has never married is busy with the Lord's work. She wants to be holy in body and spirit." This Scripture gives the best advice I know on how to get a good relationship. The instruction is simple:

While you are single, spend all of your time serving God, making Him your priority. When you do this, God has your attention, and He can guide you toward the things that are good for you. In His timing, He will speak to you about someone whom He selects for you.

It's important for you to be aware that you may or may not choose the right person for you, but God does not make mistakes. God will make it clear to you that you have found the right one if you allow Him to do the choosing for you.

Baby, I am sure that you, like most people, will sooner or later suffer a broken heart, but the frequency and intensity can be kept to a minimum by following these principles that we have talked about. But when you are hurt, know that God will always be there for you: "The Lord is close to the brokenhearted, and he saves those whose spirits have been crushed" (Psalm 34:18).

I want you to know that you can come to me and talk anytime you need to about those knuckleheaded boys. I was young once and I broke hearts and also had my heart broken. When your heart is broken, more than anything you need a listening ear. You'll always have mine.

Think About It

1. Has you heart been broken? Yes___ No___ If it has, do you feel like you're over it? Yes___ No___

2. Do you screen your dates or will you date just about anybody?

   _____

3. Regarding the last person you dated, did you plan to go out together or did it just happen?
   Planned ____
   Just happened ____

4. On a scale of 1 to 10 with 10 being the highest, how much do you love yourself? _____

5. Who is the father figure you can talk to you when your heart is broken?

   _____

   Do you contact him when you need to talk or do you suffer privately?

   _____

6. Can you quote Romans 8:28 from memory? Yes___ No___ If no, can you learn it?

7. Are you determined to have just a few relationships and not date every Tom, Jim, and Jerry?
   A few ____
   Tom, Jim, and Jerry ____

8. Find and complete this sentence: You are asking for trouble when you get into _____

Part 5

Boys Will Be Boys

21)—Games Silly Boys Play

Here's the Deal . . .

Dad notices that the phone keeps ringing, but there is no one on the line. You inform me that you think a boy is calling you and hanging up. Your dad has this advice for you.

MOST GIRLS encounter silly boys as they grow up. These boys lack the social skills needed to interact with girls in the proper way. They need time to develop those skills that will help them understand the opposite sex. When I was younger I would call girls on the phone when I really didn't have anything to say. I called simply because I was immature and enjoyed seeing how the girl would respond.

Unfortunately, there are some boys who like to play games with girls, not as a normal part of growth, but for their own warped pleasure. When you recognize that a boy's actions don't make sense, I caution you to stay alert because boys who are obviously silly don't have good intentions for you. In fact, Scripture says to, "stay away from fools, because they can't teach you anything" (Proverbs 14:7).

Some of the tactics they use in their silly games are:

1. Manipulation. The ultimate goal of manipulation is control. Silly boys want to control the girl that they are with or want to be with. They want to divert you from your designated goal in life. If you want to go to school, a silly boy will try to redirect your priorities away from getting your education. If you have decided to stay a virgin, he will make it his goal for you to lose your virginity. If you are cool, calm, and collected, he will try to make you lose your temper.

Silly boys use manipulation in all of its forms to accomplish their goal. When you see that a boy is gamin' or playin' you, dismiss him and find someone else to talk with on the phone.

2. Intimidation. Silly boys can be popular boys who use their popularity to put pressure on you. When they try to intimidate you, they are implying that there is something missing in your life. This type of boy will make it appear as though the way you have been doing things is not good enough. He wants you to doubt yourself and think that there is something wrong with you.

3. Involving a third party. Silly boys will often use the name of another girl to compare you with or to serve as competition for you. They will make statements like "so and so said this or that." The comments they make are designed to take your attention away from your commitment to be your best.

You should never let the threat of another young lady affect your decisions regarding the young man of your interest. In other words, don't work harder to get him because there is another girl in the picture. If you do this, you probably won't be able to keep him because you are not going to continue to work as hard once you get him as you did to win him. When you react to a third-party comparison, it will never help you in the long run. If you think that it is necessary to do this, it proves that your boyfriend is not very wise; in fact, he is immature and silly.

4. Sexual stimulation. Baby, don't ever allow a silly boy to talk nasty to you. If you are on the phone, hang up! If you are in a place where you can walk away from him, then do that. Boys think differently about sexual matters than girls do, especially girls who are not hood rats. A hood rat is a girl in the hood whom everybody has had sex with. This girl is very sexually active, not respected, and gets many of her needs met through sex.

When a silly boy tries to talk nasty to you, he is testing you. He wants to see how appealing sex is to you and how far he can go. Don't get involved in his silly game. Shut him off as soon as possible. If he won't leave you alone, come and tell me, and I will see to it that he won't continue to bother you. That's what dads are for.

Silly boys play games and try to manipulate girls just to see if they can get away with it. This is a ritual that they will engage in as they try to boost their egos at girls' expense. These games take many forms and are as old as mankind. The tactics boys use are easy to spot because they consist of lies and half-truths that are designed to confuse a girl and make her an easy victim.

Weak-minded girls are easy prey for the silly games that boys play. I've noticed that many TV shows have silly boys portrayed as funny and harmless. Well, in real life they are not funny, and being involved with them is no joke. The apostle Paul put it this way, "When I was a child, I talked like a child, I thought like a child, I reasoned like a child. When I became a man, I stopped those childish ways" (1 Corinthians 13:11). Silly boys have not grown up to be wise young men. They will take you down if you mix with them. That is why I am teaching you to be wise and avoid silly boys at all costs.

Think About It

1. Is there a silly boy in your life right now? Yes___ No___

2. Are you wise enough to detect a silly boy when you see one? Yes___ No___

3. Can you tell when a boy is trying to manipulate you? Yes___ No___ Why? Or why not?

Explain _____

4. Do you respond to the "he said, she said" statements that boys make? Yes___ No___ Why? Or why not?

Explain _____

5. What do you do when a boy compares you to another girl?

_____

_____

6. When you are young it is natural to be curious about sexual things. Do you allow silly boys to talk nasty to you? Yes___ No___ Why? Or why not?

Explain _____

7. What tactic do you use to shut silly boys down when they talk inappropriately to you? _____

_____

8. Write out Proverbs 14:7 so that you can memorize it:

_____

_____.

22)—Baby, You Are Always Being Watched

Here's the Deal . . .

While at the church picnic your dad observes you having a great time playing volleyball. You are oblivious to the fact that there are three young men seriously checking you out as you play. This is normal and your dad has this advice for you.

I WANT YOU to know that wherever you go, there is someone watching you. Guys love to look at young women, and for most young men it is their favorite indoor and outdoor sport. There is nothing wrong with watching women. It has been going on since the beginning of time. In fact, I was observing the sopranos in the choir one day when I first spotted your mother hitting a high note. It was love as soon as I laid eyes on her. Please note that age is not a factor. Older men look at younger women and younger men look at older women.

I can remember when you were a baby; of course, your mother was younger then. We were on campus one day taking care of some business. As your mother walked out of a room, I heard three college students say: "Man, Dr. Davis is looking gooood today!"

They were talking about your mother and my wife. They did not see me standing behind the door. When they turned around and saw me, they turned red first and then blue. I quickly thanked them for the compliment and put their minds at ease. You should consider it a compliment when men look at you, but, because of the sick society that we live in, you must also be careful.

Many men are extremely thirsty, and when they look at you, they see a cool refreshing drink. Usually when a man approaches you, sex is somewhere in his mind. If the brother has a masculine nature, then he is thinking at least a little bit about sex. This is good for you to know so that you can evaluate the various types of guys you may encounter. I want to expose three types of dudes here for you to examine.

1. Stupid dudes make crass sexual overtures. This type of brother is easy to spot because he says exactly what he is thinking. Scripture teaches that, "wise people keep what they know to themselves, but fools can't keep from showing how foolish they are" (Proverbs 12:23). A young man demonstrates foolishness when he shows he was not trained to be respectful of young ladies. So he resorts to finding pleasure for himself, and as a result, disregards the value of a young lady. Any girl who would give this brother the time of day is a fool just like he is. The boy is s-t-u-p-i-d!

2. Sincere dudes tell you that you are attractive, but that is not his primary motivation right now. The sincere young man is miles ahead of the stupid man. But don't settle for him either because you can still do better. The sincere young man knows that you are no fool, so he does not approach you like a stupid young man would. You must really be careful with guys like this because they say enough of the right things to confuse you.

This young man probably has a good relationship with his mother and sister. As a result, there exists in his mind a basic understanding and appreciation for women. In spite of this, his ultimate motive is still selfish, and he will use you if given the chance. The way you deal with a young man whom you suspect is sincere is to wait him out. Time will reveal his true motives.

ATTENTION! Young women must be able to wait young men out! You must have enough self-confidence not to fall at his feet the first time he tells you that he loves you. His plan is to get next to you by his sincere presentation, but if he is faking, he will not last long. Only young men who are truly sincere can act that way for any length of time.

Again, I say wait the young man out.

3. Smart dudes want to be your platonic (no sexual interest) friend. The smart young man knows that relationships are serious, and he gets no joy from playing with them. He does not want to become emotionally attached too soon. This young man will not have a junior high attitude about sex; so waiting will be no problem. The smart young man sees life's bigger picture and knows that bad relationships can destroy people's lives.

When you meet this type of young man, slow down, pay attention, and realize that you have an opportunity to develop a quality relationship. But before you go too far along with the relationship, ask some mature person you trust to counsel you and help you think things through.

Baby, you are always being watched, and this is how men select the women that they want to marry. The important thing to remember is, always present yourself as a lady. Ladylike behavior will attract a higher quality man than acting like a hood rat will ever attract.

Think About It

I. When you prepare to leave home in the morning, do you consider the fact that you will be watched during the day? Yes___ No___ Why? Or why not?

Explain _____

2. Do you get angry when boys casually look at you? Yes___ No___ Why? Or why not?

Explain _____

3. What do you say when stupid boys approach you?

_____

4. How do you feel when a sincere boy approaches you?

_____

5. How do you handle it when a smart boy approaches you?

_____

6. Who is the mature woman you counsel with when you need to talk about boys?

_____

7. Do you understand that you can be sexy to boys when you least expect it? Yes___ No___

8. Do you understand that a father is concerned about how you present yourself in public? Yes___ No___

23)—Don't Be a Bum Magnet

Here's the Deal . . .

While shopping in the mall, you and Dad separate to pick up some specific items. When Dad returns, I notice that a young man is talking to you. When I approach and stand beside you, the young man nods and walks away. This young man falls far below the standard that your dad has for you. As a matter of fact, I think that he is a bum. Your dad has these words of advice for you.

BABY, I HAVE known women in my day who were beautiful, talented, and smart. Because of this they could have had any man that they wanted. But do you know what? Somehow they always seemed to pick a bum to be with. Now I know that you did not have anything to do with that young man talking to you, but I just want to take this time to make a point.

When I say the word "bum," I don't mean a hobo or something like that. However, I do mean the type of person who is heading nowhere—with no education, plans, or purpose—he's just kickin' it. That's the description of a modern-day bum. Your great-grandmother called men like that "breath and britches."

The Bible identifies men who are worthless and wicked in their intentions toward unsuspecting women. Proverbs

6:12–15 says, "Some people are wicked and no good. They go around telling lies, winking with their eyes, tapping with their feet, and making signs with their fingers. They make evil plans in their hearts and are always starting arguments. So trouble will strike them in an instant; suddenly they will be so hurt no one can help them."

This mind-set has always baffled me and seemed like such a waste of energy. I have really sought to understand this behavior. And now that I am older, I think that I understand. Let me try to explain. Some bums know that they could never hook a fine young lady like you. Other bums actually believe that you would be interested in them. Let me tell you what most bums are looking for:

1. Support. Generally, this type of young man is very weak in many areas of his character and needs to draw strength from another human being to make it in life. Maybe it was his mother who messed him up by pampering him and not allowing him to grow up on his own. She provided him with so much support that he grew up to be a dependent, lazy young man. Then as he got older she was either too ashamed to continue or for some other reason was no longer able to carry him. By this time it was too late, and he had missed out on learning how to be a responsible man.

I personally know of several men who are among the sorriest men I have ever met in my life. All of them were messed up by their moms. Even now as older men, a few of them are still looking for a silly woman to support them.

2. Success. Often men will seek to advance their success in life by associating with a successful woman. Baby, you will not be happy in a relationship where you have to pull the man up. You should not be with a man who has no ambition. Men like this eventually become a weight that is too heavy to bear. I call these men "projects." Many immature women believe that they can help men change if they supply enough love and understanding. The fact of the matter is, you cannot change anybody. You can be a positive influence, but this does not guarantee that the man will change. If you hang in there with him and try to help him improve, he may or may not get better, but you will definitely pay for the effort in lost time, energy, and money.

3. Sex. There is one thing that most bums can find enough energy to do well, and that is the sex act. I have seen men who were too lazy to keep any kind of job, but could manage to keep their women pregnant. Any woman who has a man just for sex is a bum magnet because she requires nothing else from him. Think about it.

4. Sucker. There are men who live by going from woman to woman. I hate to say this, but there are some women who are suckers or bum magnets. Some women have such low self-esteem that they will accept almost any weak line from a man just to avoid being alone. Bums are good at spotting these women, and they are experts at playing them. My heart hurts for women who are suckers, but only they can decide that they would rather be alone than be used by a man. Until they are ready to make that decision, no one can help them.

How to Dispose of Bums

I. Always require something from a guy. You need to know that the young man is willing to serve you. Don't be fooled by cheap tricks and gimmicks, but make sure he is working on some long-range work plans. He should also have some proof of what he is working to accomplish.

It is easy to be kind for one day, but it is hard for a man to consistently serve a woman. The Bible indicates that a man should work to make his woman comfortable. By his actions toward her, he should make her a queen by honoring and adoring her. This Scripture gives you an idea of how the Bible says that a man should treat a woman: "A man who has just married must not be sent to war or be given any other duty. He should be free to stay home for a year to make his new wife happy" (Deuteronomy 24:5).

2. Let time be your friend. Think about this: "Love can wait to give, but lust can't wait to get." Men will sometimes shower you with kindness and affection because they know that with immature, shallow girls it does not take much to win them. Sometimes when they shower you with kindness and affection, they are trying to hurry the process of getting next to you. But I say to you, don't rush yourself. When you take the time to see if the bum is sincere, he will usually get frustrated and either pressure you or move on.

3. Make sure that you are happy being single, and don't send distress signals to a guy. If you feel that you are incomplete without someone in your life, a guy with the wrong intentions will pick up on those feelings. Young ladies can avoid feeling needy and unfulfilled by doing positive things with their time. The more you spend your time doing activities that bring you satisfaction, the more you will feel comfortable being by yourself. You won't have to rely on a steady guy to make you feel like a whole person.

Since you are a girl who has healthy self-esteem, you should know that the proper approach in dealing with a guy is to let him know that you could live with him or without him. Also keep in mind that it is only when you are married that you are connected to a man in a permanent way.

Baby, you need to get these principles in your mind because inevitably you are going to run into some guys who are bums. Dad wants you to stand tall and remember that I have prepared you to face them. If you try to get rid of a young man and he does not get the message, call me and I will come and stand beside you. I love you very much.

Think About It

I. Are you aware of the type of guy whom you attract? Yes___ No___
Why? Or why not?

Explain _____

2. Do you have strong maternal instincts and feel the need to "mother"
boys? Yes___ No___

Explain _____

3. The author tells us what most bums are looking for. Have you been
approached by any of the type of bums mentioned, and if yes, which
kind?

_____

4. There was a popular song many years ago called, "First I Look at the
Purse." This song was about men who were only interested in
women with money. Have you ever given a guy money? Yes___
No___ If so, explain why you did so.

_____

5. Do you have any weaknesses that would make you appear to be a
bum magnet? Yes___ No___ If the answer is yes, what are you
doing to correct that weakness?

_____

6. The author gives three principles under "How to Dispose of Bums."
Read the three principles again and write them here:

1. _____

2. _____

3. _____

7. Are you good at applying these three principles in your relationships? Yes___ No___ Which principle is most difficult and what are
you doing to strengthen yourself in it?_____

_____

8. What man will stand beside you and give you protection when a bum takes an interest in you? _____

_____

24 — The Man in My Baby's Life

BABY, ONE OF the greatest challenges that you will face in life is to choose the right man to be your life mate. What amazes me is that we are expected to find the right person whom we are to spend the rest of our life with at a point in life when we don't know very much about life or mates. As I reflect back on all of the girlfriends I had, one thing has become very clear to me; that is, most men do not know how to pick a woman.

As a matter of fact, I did not know how to choose a woman, and most women do know how to choose a man either. God is the only One who can truly give anyone the answer to this all-important question. But we don't readily go to Him and ask. The Bible assures us that, "if any of you needs wisdom, you should ask God for it. He is generous to everyone and will give you wisdom without criticizing you" (James 1:5). Baby, you never have to be ashamed to ask God for help.

Even though the majority of people are not good at this task, it is one of the most important decisions that you will make in your life. I have tried to treat you like a lady so that you will know what it is like to be treated the proper way, and you have come to expect it. You have seen me live with your mother all of your life, and there have been times that I have struggled with her. But in spite of my struggles, I have always treated her well. I don't want you to have any less in your life.

Where should we begin when we start talking about dating or your future mate? I believe that we must begin with how you feel about yourself. If you do not properly love and respect yourself, then that insecurity will be picked up by the men that you encounter and they may have a diminished opinion of you. This is why I encourage you to develop your relationship with Jesus so that a man will be icing on the cake and not the cake itself. No man can fully meet all of your needs; you must allow God to meet your deepest needs.

Your momma told me in the beginning of our relationship that Jesus was her number one man and that I would always be number two. This used to bother me until I developed my own relationship with Jesus to the point that He is now the number one person in my life and my wife is number two. This has worked well for us because when we were not able to meet each other's needs, Jesus was there to meet them for us.

Baby, please don't believe some of those elementary love songs where the brother is crooning about how he is going to love you from A to Z and wait on you hand and foot. I hope you realize that this is a junior high mind-set and life does not work that way. In real life, loving someone and sacrificing for them is *real hard*. This is why so many relationships don't make it and go dead after a few years.

Your mother and I started praying for your husband when you were just a little girl. We are trusting God that He will bring the right man along at the right time. You must be alert during this process because following your heart can be deceiving. Just because he is cute or has an attractive body does not mean that he is the man for you.

We have asked God to guide you; our confidence is in Him because He does not make mistakes. So you can trust God to help you choose the right mate because Scripture reminds us, "God does not see the same way people see. People look at the outside of a person, but the Lord looks at the heart" (1 Samuel 16:7).

Let me go down my list of qualifications for your future mate:

1. As a Christian, you must kick it with another Christian.
No, it does not matter how many other positive qualities he may have.
The foundation upon which the two of you will relate and build the rest
of your lives upon will be the guidelines set forth in the Word of God.
The Bible makes no distinction between races of people, but it does
make a distinction between classes of people. There are three classes of
people recognized in the Bible:

> ✿ Gentiles, or non-Christians
>
> ✿ Jewish people
>
> ✿ Christians

Each one of these groups should marry in their own class. As far as
the Bible is concerned, you are free to marry another race as long as he
is in your class. Dad's first choice would be for you to marry a man who
looks just like me but more important than that is that he must be a
Christian. Since you are a Christian, if you marry anyone other than a
Christian man, you will not be following God's plan for you.

God wants you to have the very best but you have to go about getting it His way. That's why the Bible tells us, "Do not be shaped by this
world; instead be changed within by a new way of thinking. Then you
will be able to decide what God wants for you; you will know what is
good and pleasing to him and what is perfect" (Romans 12:2).

**2. I want to know about his background and how he under-
stands it.** A person's background has to do with the home training
that he or she was given. Therefore, I am interested in the young man's
parent(s) and how they raised him. This will tell more about him than
many other factors because most young people will grow up, marry,
and duplicate the home life they came from. This is not true 100 percent
of the time, but unless young people are aware of how and where their
parents made their mistakes, they will not learn from their failures.

Kids are supposed to learn from the failures of their parents. If the
boy's background and upbringing was not good, he can always correct
the mistakes that were made if he is aware of the problems and willing
to change. At some point the both of you need to discuss how you plan
to overcome the character defects and bad habits you learned from your
parents. Finally, as your relationship begins to develop, be sure to meet
his mom and dad and have a long talk with them.

3. I want to know about his ambitions. What are his future plans, and what has he already done to make them a reality? You should look at his record and see if he has accomplished anything positive at this point in his life. Many boys wait until they meet a woman before they decide to do something with their lives. This is not a good sign because he needs to be self-motivated and already have established some goals for himself. Inquire about his school record. It he is not interested in school, that does not speak well for his future.

Also, find out what he owns and who paid for it. If his parents purchased everything he has, you may have a young man who will look for women to take care of him. You need to learn to spot boys like this at an early age before you find yourself stuck with one.

4. I want to know if he is in a rush to develop a relationship. When guys are in a rush to get the relationship going, it is usually a bad sign. If he has good intentions, then he is usually willing to take his time. The only way to really know certain things is to take some time. Time is the only way to see a man's true colors. It is easy to put on an act for a few months, but when boys are forced to wait one or two years, you generally have a better chance to see what he is made of. You may think that is a long time, but two short years are nothing compared to a lifetime of bad feelings and memories.

5. I want to know who the men are in the boy's life. Every young man needs some men in his life to guide him as he tries to build and lead a family. If his only friends and advisors are his "homies," then watch out. What is his attitude regarding older men? Is he mature enough to appreciate their wisdom and guidance, or is he rebellious and rejects the wisdom of experience?

6. Be sure to read the Bible with him. This will also help expose what he is really made of. If you listen to God, God will help you determine if the young man is the right one for you simply by following what the Scripture says. "God's word is alive and working and is sharper than a double-edged sword. It cuts all the way into us, where the soul and the spirit are joined, to the center of our joints and bones. And it judges the thoughts and feelings in our hearts" (Hebrews 4:12). It would be very difficult for someone to read the Bible with you and smile when he does not have good intentions. If he won't read the Bible and go to church with you now, what makes you think he will do it later after you are married and have kids? No one can hide from the truth of the Bible.

This is the main reason for marrying someone who is a Christian. The Bible is very clear in saying, "You are not the same as those who do not believe. So do not join yourselves to them. Good and bad do not belong together. Light and darkness cannot share together" (2 Corinthians 6:14). This is the commandment of God, and we must obey it to stay in right standing with Him. You can save yourself a lot of heartache by doing what the Bible tells you.

There are many qualities and conditions that I could list about your future man, and these are just a few. I must also mention that I have tried to raise you in a manner in which you are not starving for a relationship with a man. It would hurt me deeply to think that you were chasing men. You should be attentive to men but never chase them or feel like you cannot live without one. Even if you don't get a man, never stoop so low as to chase after one.

The Bible clearly teaches that the man should start the relationship. Proverbs 18:22 states, "When a man finds a wife, he finds something good. It shows that the Lord is pleased with him." The Bible does not say that the woman who finds a man finds a good thing. Baby, Dad wants you to make sure that you keep a healthy perspective about who you are and wait on God to send the mate for you. Until then, Jesus, along with me, your brother, and the rest of the family will work to keep your mind occupied until God sends that right one along.

Think About It

1. If you have a relationship with your father, good or bad, how do you feel that it influences the type of boys you are attracted to?

   _____

2. Do you feel that you must have a man to be satisfied in life? Yes___ No___ Why? Or why not?

   Explain _____

3. In the second sentence of this chapter the author says that he is amazed by something. What is it?

   _____

4. What are you doing right now to prepare yourself for your future husband?

   _____

   _____

5. The author lists six qualifications that he is concerned about. From your perspective, what qualifications did he leave out?

   _____

6. How do you rate your maturity level in choosing boys?

   Not mature ___

   Mature ___

   Very mature ___

7. Who should initiate the relationship, the man or woman?

   _____

8. Describe what you think the perfect man looks like.

   _____

25)—Baby, He's Too Old!

Here's the Deal . . .

While riding in the car together we see a well-built man jogging down the street. I wave at him because he is a business acquaintance of mine. You ask: "Who was that?" Sensing your interest, I respond with these comments.

WHAT DO OLDER men want with younger women? Why are they dissatisfied with women their own age? Well, from a father's perspective, all of the reasons are negative. Before a young girl should even consider dating an older man, she should investigate the situation as thoroughly as possible. A girl should want to know if a man genuinely has an interest in her or if he is just playing on her youthful ignorance. Even though this is true, it is possible that an older man could really love a younger lady and would make a wonderful husband. But, as a concerned parent I would be very cautious about consenting to such a marriage.

Because so many young men are going to prison and others are wasting prime time with drug abuse, older men are an issue that we must seriously consider. The real concern is not how old he is but what type of person he might be. Therefore, a girl needs to find out as much as she can about his background before becoming involved with an older man. When the brother is older there are some important questions that need to be answered. You should immediately ask yourself:

❀ Why doesn't he have a woman already?

❀ Is he a mommy's boy?

❀ Is he a man who formerly preferred men and wants to come back to women?

❀ Is he afraid of commitment?

❀ Does he have a family already?

❀ Is he not up to the challenge of a mature woman his own age?

Although Dad has trained you regarding how men think, I still will not allow you to go head-to-head with a man who is much older than you are. This is especially true if I am not sure about his intentions. Wisdom is acquired with age and life experience. Older men can rush younger women and cause them to miss out on many valuable experiences because they have already lived through them. For example, your mother and I had to learn about having a family together. All of the struggles of being young and newly married were unfamiliar and challenging to both of us. When you marry someone who has "been there and done that," it could steal some of the joy out of your early years of marriage.

On the other hand, an older man may be settled and mature enough to guide you better than a younger, less experienced man. But this type of man has a rare expression of love and commitment; men of this caliber don't come along too often. Generally speaking, I don't want you kickin' it with an older man. That's just my preference.

I know that you are not pleased with my decision, but I am going to remind you again that you are Daddy's prize, my joy, my heart—all that and much more. I am not going to let any young man get next to you who has questionable intentions and an unfair advantage over you.

Men must also be careful about their motives when they are attracted to younger women because they may be trying to recapture their youth and innocence again. This is not possible, and their behavior could be harmful to you in the long run. I stated earlier that they may not be up to the challenge of having a woman of their own age. For example, I can tell you that your mother is a mental challenge for me because her life experience is similar to mine. This means that we have something in common. On the other hand, a younger woman would be no match for me mentally because of the level of wisdom and knowledge I have acquired over the years.

Young girls who are attracted to older men need to consider the reasons for their attraction to see if they are looking for a daddy replacement. It is common for some females to look for their father's characteristics in a man they are considering for a mate. At the same time, it's really a bad thing when young ladies look for older men to be their sugar daddies, which means the men are a constant source of money for them. In either case, some self-examination is in order for women to determine their motives about the men they choose.

Finally, I suggest that any girl who wants to date an older man get some counseling from her wisest, most mature friends and proceed slowly with the relationship. A smart young lady will also want to take advantage of help that loved ones will offer her. Proverbs 19:20 offers some sound instruction to follow: "Listen to advice and accept correction, and in the end you will be wise." We can all benefit from having wisdom to guide us through life's important decisions. The Bible has declared God's wisdom to be the main ingredient of a successful life in Christ.

As your dad, my preference is that you find a young man your age who loves you and wants to grow old with you. This is because I love you with all of my heart and I want God's plan to be fulfilled for you. I think that the Bible says it best: "My child, listen to your father's teaching and do not forget your mother's advice" (Proverbs 1:8).

Think About It

I. Have you ever been attracted to an older guy? Yes___ No___ If yes, how much older?_____

2. Has an older guy ever asked you for your phone number or a date? Yes___ No___

3. What are some of the positive factors the author named for dating an older man?

_____

4. What are some of the negative factors the author named for dating an older man?

_____

5. What do you think girls see in older guys?

_____

6. Are you impressed with the material things (apartment, nice wheels, clothes, cash in the pocket) that a guy has? Yes___ No___

7. Do you have friends who date older guys? Yes___ No___

8. Do you feel that older guys push you to have sex more than younger guys? Yes___ No___

9. As you get older, age becomes less of a factor but for you right now, how old is too old? _____

IO. The author had a real attitude about his daughter dating an older dude. Do you think he was right or wrong? _____

_____

Part 6

Can Dad Love Me?

26)—My Dad Has Another Family Now

BECAUSE OF THE high rate of divorce, there are many dads who are responsible for two sets of kids. Whenever this occurs it can be very painful for all involved. A forty-eight-year-old woman from Chicago made this personal observation: "I love him but learned early not to depend on him for certain things. He is nice but closer to his second family than to me and my brothers. He did the best he knew how to do. He does not know that he hurt us so much."

The pain of parental separation is devastating to children, particularly when they are forced to compete with other children for their father's attention. The practice of a man having multiple families is not God's plan, and that is why it has never worked well. If your dad has another family, I want you to consider these things:

I. He is probably stretched to the limit. A man who has two sets of children will most likely try to please both families. As a result he could find himself being stretched physically, mentally, spiritually, financially, emotionally, and in all other ways. Wisdom says that to put demands on him at this time may be a wasted effort.

2. The consequences of his actions will follow him for the rest of his life. I personally know many men who regret leaving their first family, but it is too late to go back to them. As men get older and wiser they often suffer mental anguish over their decision to leave their first home to start a new life and family.

3. Don't hate the other family. No one is a winner in this situation. Because your dad is there with them now does not mean that they have won and you've lost. Don't feel forced to love them or treat them like family. If you befriend your half brothers and sisters that's OK, but if you find that you cannot, don't feel guilty about it. Remember that all of the kids involved are innocent victims. Don't blame them. God is the ultimate judge, and He will settle all issues in His own time. If you stoop so low as to hate the other family, it will only hurt you in the end.

4. When you see or talk to him, assume that he is hurting also. Even if he smiles and puts on a good show, assume that Dad is hurting. I know that this sounds crazy, but you need to try to be the strong one. Think about it this way: if your dad left your family, you know that he needs prayer. If his mind was on Jesus, and he was being obedient to Jesus, he would have stayed at home. Well, since he did not stay at home, we can assume that spiritually he is hurting. Pray for him.

Pledge now that you will have a "no divorce" clause in your wedding ceremony. To help avoid divorce or separation in the future, determine to get premarital counseling before you get married. Promise yourself now that you will not marry a brother who is shaky in the beginning of your relationship. Of all the couples I have married, there is only one couple I regret marrying. When I look back, the brother was shaky from the beginning. Promise to only marry a brother who has a solid character, and ask God to help you fulfill that desire.

Talk to Your Heavenly Father

PSALM 27:10 has given us the assurance that God will be the parent that we need. Remember to quote this Scripture when you feel the lack of your father's presence: "If my father and mother leave me, the Lord will take me in."

In your own words, write how you feel about your father's absence from your home because he lives with another family. Tell God how you feel about not having your father in your daily life by recording your thoughts below.

_____

_____

_____

_____

_____

_____

_____

_____

_____

_____

_____

_____

_____

_____

_____

_____

_____

27)—My Dad Is Abusive to Mom

THERE ARE MANY ways that a dad can abuse a mom. I believe that giving her the silent treatment would be considered one of the simplest ways of mistreating her. Men can punish women by tuning them out mentally; for example, like being in the same house and not acknowledging her or speaking to her.

Unfortunately there are other forms of abuse that are not so subtle. God knows the pain when a husband and wife yell at each other, shouting obscenities while the children watch. Things become even worse when Dad becomes physical with Mom and causes bodily harm to her. Far too many children have terrible memories of Mom and Dad's heated arguments that haunt them well into the adult years.

God's design for a husband and wife can be found in Ephesians 5:33: "Each one of you must love his wife as he loves himself, and a wife must respect her husband."

The pain of abusive fathers is very real in the day-to-day life of children and in the memories of adults who struggle to make sense of it all. I want you to know that the root of all abuse is sin. I know that this sounds like a simplified answer, but it is the correct answer. Fathers who have not given their lives to the Lord Jesus Christ are slaves to sin, and they are influenced by the Evil One.

Prayer is always in order for abusive dads. The Bible tells us to pray for people who cause us pain. Here are some Scriptures that can remind you to pray for your dad.

"Bless those who curse you, pray for those who are cruel to you" (Luke 6:28).

"Pray for those who hurt you" (Matthew 5:44).

"Always be joyful. Pray continually, and give thanks whatever happens. That is what God wants for you in Christ Jesus" (1 Thessalonians 5:16–18).

Let me share with you some reasons why some men are abusive:

I. They were abused in their childhood. Listen to this comment from a forty-one-year-old Chicago woman: "I realize now that much of my father's abusive behavior toward my mom was the result of his being abused as a child. I did not understand this when I was growing up and harbored much bitterness and resentment toward him. It is so important that we as the body of Christ work to break the vicious cycle of violence and abuse that begins with our childhood and continues into adulthood."

Begin to pray and ask God to help you stop the cycle of abuse with your generation. With God's help, you can do it. Remember to believe what the Bible has claimed for you: "I can do all things through Christ, because he gives me strength" (Philippians 4:13).

It is a good thing to have someone close to you whom you can trust and confide in. Ask God to give you a friend you can talk to about your pain.

2. They abuse women because of jealousy. That's right! They are jealous of the woman's strength, intelligence, and ability to survive in this world. Some sick men see women as possessing strength because they are the mothers and wives who at times demonstrate great power in their everyday lives. Also, some sick men are jealous of women because of their attractiveness and the attention they receive from other men.

3. They abuse women because they have not learned how to deal with their frustrations in any other way. With the growing epidemic of absentee fathers and domestic violence being portrayed in the media, it is no wonder that many men are abusing women. To counteract this growing problem, the church must develop more seminars and men's groups where the older, wiser men can teach the younger men how to treat women with respect and honor.

There are many other reasons why men abuse women. I believe that the challenge for a girl who grew up with a father who abused her mother would be to ask God to give her a proper perspective on her situation. God is the only One who can heal the pain caused by domestic abuse, so it stands to reason that we must turn to Him for His help in resolving matters of abuse.

Unfortunately, many girls who have abusive fathers go to one of two extremes:

1. They may show uncontrolled feelings of hatred toward boys and give all of their male acquaintances a hard time.

2. They lose all self-control the first time they meet a kind, gentle young man and will do almost anything to keep him.

Either extreme is bad. The key is to find a balance between the two extremes. You must first recognize where you are mentally and emotionally. This is not always easy for someone to do. It may require you to ask for the guidance of a compassionate and experienced adult to help pray you through the process of releasing ill feelings toward your father figure.

Talk to Your Heavenly Father

GOD WANTS YOU to forgive your father in spite of what he has done. This is because God intends to correct all wrongs in His own timing. We must be careful to do our part and obey God's Word and trust that He will work things out. Follow Ephesians 4:32 and watch God work on your behalf: "Be kind and loving to each other, and forgive each other just as God forgave you in Christ."

In your own words, write how you feel about your father's abusive behavior. Also write a prayer that you can pray daily for your father to overcome his problem.

_____

_____

_____

_____

_____

_____

_____

_____

_____

_____

_____

_____

_____

_____

_____

_____

_____

28 — I Feel Insecure and Unloved

IT HAS BEEN PROVEN by many studies that girls who don't have fathers in their lives often feel insecure or unloved. This may also be true of fathers who are present but do not have loving interactions with their daughters. A thirty-five-year-old California woman shared her feelings on this concept: "My dad has always been a part of my life, but he's a very passive and quiet man. We've never sat down for a length of time to talk. If I remember correctly, he's never hugged me or told me that he loves me."

Feelings of insecurity or of being unloved can be common among young ladies who have fathers and also young ladies who don't have fathers. What I find very interesting is that psychologists suggest that, as humans, we all have two basic needs:

1. The need to feel significant or important.
2. The need to feel secure.

When people—men or women—do not have these basic needs met, it will often be acted out in their behavior. When the father/daughter relationship is not healthy, young ladies have an empty place in their lives. If you occasionally suffer from feelings of insecurity or of being unloved, here are some suggestions for you to follow.

1. Learn to let Jesus meet your basic needs for significance and security. The fact of the matter is that no human being can adequately meet the needs of another person. I have always appreciated my wife because she has a strong relationship with Christ that provides her with a supernatural hookup. All I had to do was to supply the human hookup, which was not beyond my ability. The problem comes when women do not have a supernatural hookup with God and they un-knowingly expect too much from the man in their life.

2. Don't hide your feelings of loneliness. It is very healthy to talk about your feelings with a friend. When you talk them through, consider the good with the bad, and you will discover that the good will always outweigh the bad. When you give your feelings to God, He will help you to realize you are who the Bible says you are: "In all these things we are completely victorious through God who showed his love for us" (Romans 8:37).

3. Compare your problem with the problems that some young women have. Generally, this will help you see that your situa-tion is not as bad as you thought it was after all. You will always be able to hear stories of people who have problems and are presently suf-fering under conditions that are far worse than your own. When you think about this, it will give you a better perspective as you consider their situations. What others have to endure is often unbearable in com-parison to your own problems.

4. Ask God to provide you with a source of fatherly influ-ence. God knows your needs even before you ask Him. When we pray and ask Him to do something, it must be something that is within His will for our lives. That's why it's so important to ask Him; it helps us to focus on what God wants for us. If you tell God that you need someone to fill the empty space where a father's love would occupy, He will give you exactly what you need.

So open up your heart and talk to God. He will hear your prayer of faith and honor it by responding with the answer that you need the most. Just remember that God's answer doesn't always look like what we are expecting it to. Be open to what God will provide for you as an answer to your need. The Word of God tells us, "And if (since) we [pos-itively] know that He listens to us in whatever we ask, we also know [with settled and absolute knowledge] that we have [granted us as our present possessions] the requests made of Him" (1 John 5:15 AMP).

5. Realize that ultimately, God is your Father. In the final analysis, God is your true Father. Listen to what this thirty-four-year-old woman from California said about her absent father: "God has been the father to me that my father does not know how to be. My dad is ir-responsible, fearful, detached, and inconsistent; he is not a promise keeper. I hope that he will give his life to God. Only God can fix him. I know some of the scars it has caused (sexual activity, low self-esteem) but God is faithful. He is healing every single thing. I love my father and my heavenly Father, but God can respond when my father can't."

I want you to be proactive in accepting the reality that is described here. These are some things you can do that can make a difference in your attitude and your actions. It all starts with bringing God into your confidence and trusting Him to work on your behalf. There is no reason for you to suffer needlessly, and you won't when God is on your side.

Talk to Your Heavenly Father

SECOND CORINTHIANS 13:11 assures you that "the God of love and peace will be with you." In your own words, describe your insecurities in detail. Also express to God how it feels when you think you are not loved. God will listen to your heart's cry and comfort you with His love and surround you with His peace.

_____

_____

_____

_____

_____

_____

_____

_____

_____

_____

_____

_____

_____

_____

_____

_____

_____

_____

29)—My Dad Needs to Apologize for How He Hurt Me

IN OUR MINDS and hearts we know that things should go a certain way. We see situations where other people seem to have it together and wonder why we could not have had it that way. There are many young ladies who are waiting for their dad to try to fix all of the pain that he has caused. In the backs of their minds they keep telling themselves that *he needs to say he's sorry*.

Unfortunately, it is possible that he will never say that he is sorry. He may never actually come to you and apologize for the pain he has caused in your life. A thirty-four-year-old woman from Chicago stated that she wanted her father to tell her that he was sorry for not being a committed and honest father. She felt that he should show regret for not being there for his family. She wanted him to apologize for being irresponsible and for acting out his frustrations on them by being an alcoholic.

It is normal to desire a good relationship with your father. But the pain that is felt when you consider that he is the cause of your family's instability will occasionally make you angry. I agree that God did not plan it that way, but because of the decisions that your dad made, you are hurt and you want him to apologize. As you work through your emotions, I pray that the following ideas will be a source of help in making you a strong young woman:

1. Don't wait for your dad to come around; go on with your life. If you are waiting for an apology, you are carrying unnecessary emotional baggage. You are looking at the past, carrying unnecessary past pain, and hoping for a miracle. This is not a wise way to spend your life. You may be unconsciously expecting your personal sense of happiness and well-being to come from another human who cannot provide it for you.

Learn to be independent of those counterproductive thoughts by focusing your attention on the Word of God, "forgetting those things which are behind and reaching forward to those things which are ahead" (Philippians 3:13 NKJV). If you practice modeling this behavior, you will soon find it easier to leave the past behind you and focus your thoughts on having a bright future. Develop the attitude that if he comes around and wants to fix your relationship by saying that he is sorry, then that's OK. If not, keep telling yourself: "I'll still rise."

2. Even if your dad does come around and says, "I'm sorry," he can't undo the past. Past memories never go away. The mind has them stored away in secret compartments. You may be able to develop a decent relationship, but you will still face the challenge of forgiving him for the past. That same thirty-four-year-old woman from Chicago made this statement: "My father and I had a poor relationship growing up. It is better today, but I still feel very uncomfortable with him, and I really blame him for causing me to have so much confusion in my life today with relationships, with men particularly, but also with people in general."

Reconciliation is never easy and can only be done with God's help. The pain of the past can only be dealt with by keeping your focus on God and looking to the future.

3. Dump all of your anger for your dad onto Jesus. Actually, that is why Jesus is with us. He wants to take your hurts and pains and replace them with His love. God's Word assures us that this is what we should do: "Give all your worries to him, because he cares about you" (1 Peter 5:7).

I used to hear old folks say this, and I did not understand it. Now that I am an adult, I understand it. Don't try to understand it right away; just do it and have faith that God will respond to you. Say something like this: "Dear Jesus, my dad has really hurt me. I want You to take this hurt. I give it to You now. Please replace this hurt with Your joy. In Your name, I pray. Amen." This may have to be a daily confession, but keep giving it to Jesus as many times as necessary, and as time passes your healing is sure to happen.

Talk to Your Heavenly Father

IN YOUR OWN WORDS, tell God about the hurt your father has caused you. Write a prayer asking God to help you forgive your father. If you ever wonder if you can forgive him, always remember that the Word of God has the answer you are looking for: "Yes, if you forgive others for their sins, your Father in heaven will also forgive you for your sins. But if you don't forgive others, your Father in heaven will not forgive your sins" (Matthew 6:14–15).

_____

_____

_____

_____

_____

_____

_____

_____

_____

_____

_____

_____

_____

_____

_____

_____

_____

_____

30)—My Dad Is Dead

WHEN DEATH TAKES a good father out of a home, the family usually feels robbed. The sense of loss can be overwhelming. The hole that is left seems to draw everything into it and create an inescapable world of pain. A twenty-six-year-old young lady from Florida made this observation: "My father is now deceased. I miss his wise words, and it often makes me feel empty."

It is times like this when people look to God for answers. The Bible teaches that we never cease to exist. We just change forms and locations. When a Christian dies, our new location becomes heaven. This is why the decision to accept Christ and the free gift of salvation is the most important choice we have to make in life. Unfortunately, when a non-Christian dies, the Bible teaches that their new location becomes that place of outer darkness called hell. Therefore, if your father accepted the Lord Jesus Christ at some point in his life, it is only a matter of time before you will see you him again.

When a loved one dies, the role of the church family and friends is to comfort the family members who have suffered the loss. This is always a good time to spend some time evaluating your life and to draw strength from the Lord to carry on with your future. Read the following descriptions and reflect on those that touch your life. Share your feelings on these subjects with God, and ask Him to help you to move on.

I. You may have unresolved issues with your dad. He is no longer alive, but there are still some things you did not have the opportunity to talk over with him. These issues will remain unsettled in your heart until you confront them. I suggest that you make a list of the things you need to resolve with your dad. Find a convenient time to be alone in a place where he frequently spent time, such as his favorite chair or his seat at the dinner table. Pretend that he is there with you and listening to your every word. You can then pour out your heart and tell him all that you wanted him to know. This exercise should help you feel better and bring some closure to your concerns.

2. There is an emptiness in your life that makes you feel incomplete. When death takes someone from us, we all experience a sense of being incomplete. I suggest that you talk openly with your loved ones and commit to support one another by talking out your feelings and listening to others.

Prayer can also help get you through the difficult times. So spend more time talking to God and sharing your feelings with Him. You can tell God things that you might not feel comfortable sharing with other people. If you think you do not know how to pray, you should know that prayer is simply communicating with God. Imagine God is the other person in the room with you, and just talk with Him in the same way you would talk with another human being.

Don't worry about it; God can interpret your true feelings; He knows what is in your heart. You may be surprised at how talking openly about your thoughts really helps you to deal with the empty feelings inside of you.

3. Become more aggressive in reaching your goals in life. The loss of a parent, no matter what your age, can make an individual feel like an orphan. A sixty-five-year-old woman from Chicago stated: "My dad died when I was fifty-nine years old and I still miss him." To keep your mind occupied and to prepare you for your future, get busy making your dreams come true. This will occupy your mind with positive ideas while it also prepares you for the next steps for you to take toward your future.

4. Help somebody else in need. I am amazed at how quickly we begin to feel better when we stop to help other people. This is part of the biblical principle called reaping what you sow: "Give, and you will receive. You will be given much. Pressed down, shaken together, and running over, it will spill into your lap. The way you give to others is the way God will give to you" (Luke 6:38). This means if you are kind to people in need, someone will be kind to you in your time of need.

The process of mourning for a loved one is very normal and necessary for a period of time. However, it is not healthy for it to go on indefinitely. Memories will remain, and you will think about your dad from time to time. But avoid dwelling on what could have or should have been.

The key is not to focus on death but to keep your mind on living your life in a way that is pleasing to God. God wants you to forgive your father for whatever hurt he caused you. He also wants you to focus on Him and the plans He has in store for you. The only way you will learn more about God and His purpose for your life is to learn more about God's Word. You can do that by attending a good Bible study where people are eager and hungry to understand the Word of God. You will be amazed at how quickly you will grow and how your ability to cope with the loss of your dad will improve.

Talk to Your Heavenly Father

IN YOUR OWN WORDS, describe your feelings about the loss of your father. Pour out your heart and express to God what you need from Him to help you better cope with your father's death. You can claim the blessing that Matthew 5:4 shares for those who have lost a loved one: "They are blessed who grieve, for God will comfort them."

_____

_____

_____

_____

_____

_____

_____

_____

_____

_____

_____

_____

_____

_____

_____

_____

_____

_____

_____

_____

31)—My Dad Has a Bad Habit
(Taking the Good with the Bad)

MANY YOUNG GIRLS are born with a father who may have a weakness that strains their relationship and puts pressure on the family overall. A twenty-four-year-old woman from Florida had these comments about her father: "My father did give us some memorable moments, yet the alcoholism was always around, which led to possessiveness." This young lady was faced with the dilemma of taking the good along with the bad. Her dad would sometimes do good things. However, because of his alcoholism his behavior was unpredictable and often disappointing.

In the family structure, Dad is supposed to be a protector, a provider, and a pal. Unfortunately, this is not the case in many situations. If your dad does goods things for the family but also does bad things because of a negative habit, here are some things you should remember:

I. Always try to separate your dad's actions from his intentions. Sin is a powerful influence in the life of a father who has a weakness. That father can love his children greatly, and with all of his heart he may want the best for them. In spite of his good intentions, he may not have the spiritual strength to overcome his area of weakness. The apostle Paul understood this dilemma and wrote about it: "I do not do the good things I want to do, but I do the bad things I do not want to do" (Romans 7:19).

Because of circumstances beyond their control, there are men who have difficulty coping with life. These men respond to life's challenges in various ways, such as using drugs, running away from responsibilities, or having violent behavior. Worse yet, these actions often take them away from their families and send them to prison. Men who find themselves in such negative circumstances cannot deal with family pressures and are looking for an escape. If your dad is weak and acts out negative behaviors, take pride in his good intentions and ask God to help you for-give his wrong actions.

2. Remember that your dad can change for the better at any time. I have had the privilege of participating in the rehabilitation of many men whom society has given up on. Some of these men were in their thirties, forties, and even their fifties when they began to look for help. So I am a witness and can say for sure that it is never too late to change. As long as your dad is still alive, he has the opportunity to change.

My concern for you is that you do not base your life and happiness on the hope that he *will* change. He may or may not change his ways. Your personal happiness cannot be based on his decisions about his personal life. God has the answer for Dad's needs, but Dad has to do something. I share this Scripture with men who want to change their lives for the better. God says, "'Pray to me, and I will answer you. I will tell you important secrets you have never heard before'" (Jeremiah 33:3). You see, Dad must call on God for help. Neither you nor anyone else can do it for him. What you can do is pray to God, asking Him to draw your father to Himself. God can hear your prayers and touch your dad's heart, making him aware that he needs to change. It's then up to your father to reach out to God.

3. Remember that you play a crucial role in your father's life. The phrase "standing in the gap" is becoming popular these days. This phrase is found in the New King James Version of the following Scripture, which says: "So I sought for a man among them who would make a wall, and stand in the gap before Me on behalf of the land, that I should not destroy it; but I found no one" (Ezekiel 22:30).

The "gap" represents a vulnerable space in your dad's life that he cannot defend because it is influenced by sin. If the Devil takes control of that gap, he will have access to your dad and can try to destroy him. You can ask God to take control of that space through your prayers. When you pray for your dad, you are standing in the gap for him.

I know of a man who was using heroin every day for many years. His two daughters prayed unceasingly for him, which means that they stood in the gap for him. Now this man is currently living a model life and helping other young men get their lives together. Let me ask you this: Are you praying for your dad or are you just complaining about him? The Bible says to, "Confess your sins to each other and pray for each other so God can heal you. When a believing person prays, great things happen" (James 5:16).

It may be difficult to immediately stop complaining about your dad, but remember to balance the time you complain about him with the same amount of time that you pray for him. If you pray diligently, the time that you used to complain will begin to be reduced. The key is to not give up. Prayer will change things. First of all, prayer changes you. It calms you and helps you to accept God's plan and perspective. It will be easier to see problems and disappointments from God's viewpoint after you have prayed.

Talk to Your Heavenly Father

GOD WANTS YOU to give your concerns about your dad to Him because He is the One who has the power to change things. In the meantime, put your trust in Him and know that He has not forgotten about your needs. Follow God's Word and believe that He has your best interests in mind: "Do not worry about anything, but pray and ask God for everything you need, always giving thanks. And God's peace, which is so great we cannot understand it, will keep your hearts and minds in Christ Jesus" (Philippians 4:6–7).

In your own words, describe your feelings about how your dad's bad habit has affected your life. Pour out your heart and express to God what you need from Him to help you better cope with your father's weakness. Also write out some ways that you will work to improve your own life and prepare for your future.

_____

_____

_____

_____

_____

_____

_____

_____

_____

_____

_____

_____

_____

_____

_____

32)—My Dad Is Great!

WE HEAR SO MUCH negative talk about dads, especially Black dads, that we may forget that there are actually some fantastic fathers out there. There are young girls who have no idea what it is like to be yelled at or mistreated in any way. These girls are "spoiled rotten," as the saying goes, by a dad who stands right next to God in the eyes of his daughters. Girls who have fathers like this have a great foundation on which to build their lives. Many dads have prayed prayers for their children just like Job from the Bible prayed for his children every day.

If you have a great dad, there are some things that you should consider:

1. Don't hurt him by doing something stupid with young men. Men understand young men. Men know what young men want and how they think. You are your dad's choice possession, and he wants you to have a young man who will love you totally and commit to a lifetime of togetherness. Your dad knows how a young man changes with time. There is a huge difference between a young boy of sixteen and that same young man when he reaches twenty-six.

When your father thinks about boys, he considers this and many other factors. The bottom line is, talk to your dad about young men. Depending on the type of relationship you have with your father, on one hand your style of communication may be easy and laid-back. But on the other hand, he may be unable to have open and comfortable conversations with you about boys. If he seems hesitant about talking, let him know how much it would mean to you if he were to share his wisdom with you.

2. Dress modestly. Don't go out of the house with a lot of your body exposed. This disrespects Dad in a *big* way. Dad knows how boys respond to that type of dress. He also knows that you are only asking for trouble. Boys will spend all of their time trying to figure out how to get next to you when you dress in skimpy clothing. If you do not know what skimpy clothing is, ask your dad or someone else whose opinion you trust, and he or she will tell you.

3. Use all of the wisdom that he has taught you. Throughout your life, your dad has taught you and prepared you to face the world. Make him proud by acting wisely.

4. Look your dad in the eye and tell him that he is a good dad. Actually, this is one of the greatest compliments you can give him. Telling your dad how much you appreciate him is the most priceless gift that you can give him.

Be patient as he releases you to adulthood. For the last sixteen years or so, your dad has watched over you daily, with his thoughts on you while you were out of his sight. Now he must learn to let you stay out later and be patient with you as you make more of your daily decisions. Basically, he has to learn how to release you to adulthood. If you are a first child, this will be especially difficult for him. But regardless of which child you are, releasing you is a time of transition for your dad, just as it is for you. Be patient with him. Offer him frequent reports on your life so he will know how you are doing without having to ask.

Finally, pray for him daily because he has never been as old as he is now and has never faced the challenges in life that he is now facing. The Word of God has wisely summed up how the generations relate to one another by saying, "Old people are proud of their grandchildren, and children are proud of their parents" (Proverbs 17:6).

Talk to Your Heavenly Father

SCRIPTURE SAYS: "Always give thanks to God the Father for everything, in the name of our Lord Jesus Christ" (Ephesians 5:20). You have a very good reason to give God thanks for how He has blessed your life with a great father.

In your own words, tell God how much you appreciate the fact that He gave you a wonderful father who loves you very much. After you have expressed your feelings to God about this, be sure to make it a point to tell your dad how much you love and appreciate him.

_____

_____

_____

_____

_____

_____

_____

_____

_____

_____

_____

_____

_____

_____

_____

_____

Part 7

God Is Your Father

33)—Relating to Your Heavenly Father

I AM VERY CONCERNED about the number of young women who have lost respect for their fathers. Much of the media speaks negatively of fatherhood. I am also concerned that some girls do not see God as a loving heavenly Father, but as a mean, restricting Lord they must serve.

Many young ladies have had the terrible experience of being the daughter of a father who did not treat them right. There may have been other men to assist them, but it was not their biological father who gave them guidance and protection. Because of a lack of nurturing from their fathers, some girls suffer from feelings of low self-esteem, abandonment, and insecurity.

Their experiences result in pain that is handled in various ways.

- ✢ Some girls pretend that they are totally self-sufficient and did not miss the love of their father.
- ✢ Some girls suppress their pain of rejection and do not deal with their true feelings.
- ✢ Some girls are hostile toward all men and reject the concept of fatherhood.
- ✢ Some girls go from man to man seeking to fill the void that her father left.

I want you to realize that no person alive is responsible for the circumstances surrounding their birth. The type of family that we are born into is totally out of our control. At the same time, once we grow up, we are truly blessed when we overcome the negative aspects of our family history. It takes the power of God to prevent our backgrounds from having control over us and negatively affecting our attitudes.

People who are well adjusted to life understand that when they have suffered abuse at the hands of another person, it does not indict or implicate all people with similar characteristics. For example, I have a close friend whose fourth grade teacher had red hair and constantly dogged her out. Since then she has struggled for years with her attitude toward redheaded people. Now, we know that all redheaded people are not bad, but because of her experience she struggles in that area. I know another lady who was molested by a tall, dark-skinned man. Even though it was years ago, she has never dated a tall, dark-skinned man.

The point I am trying to make is that if you are disappointed with your biological father, you should not transfer that disappointment to our Father in heaven! Instead, you will be blessed beyond measure if you work diligently to develop a healthy attitude toward our Father God. I know that this can be difficult if you are a girl who has been greatly disappointed by your dad and even now feel the pain from that relationship. The danger here is that you must not transfer your frustration with your earthly father to your heavenly Father if you want to live a healthy and happy life. God wants His children to live healthy lives filled with love and happiness.

The image of God as a loving and benevolent Father is a concept that is found in the Bible from cover to cover. I guess the most famous passage is taken from Matthew 6:9, 11, which addresses God this way: "Our Father in heaven, may your name always be kept holy. . . . Give us the food we need for each day."

A loving biological father should desire to imitate God in the love that he shows to his children. As a matter of fact, the Bible approaches fatherly love from two perspectives. Consider these Scriptures:

The Heavenly Father Used as a Model of Love

I. The Bible says that men should imitate the way that God fathers us. In Matthew 7:11 Jesus said to the people, "You know how to give good gifts to your children. How much more your heavenly Father will give good things to those who ask him!"

1 Peter 5:7 refers to God's loving care for His children and is a reminder to "give all your worries to him, because he cares about you."

Hebrews 2:6 recognizes God's care for His children by identifying two crucial questions directed toward Him: "It is written in the Scriptures, 'Why are people even important to you? Why do you take care of human beings?'"

2. The Bible shows the earthly father how to model the way that the heavenly Father loves us. Matthew 6:26 describes how the heavenly Father loves us by pointing out how He takes cares of the things of nature: "Look at the birds in the air. They don't plant or harvest or store food in barns, but your heavenly Father feeds them. And you know that you are worth much more than the birds."

This Scripture shows how God feeds the birds; He meets their needs. If He feeds the birds, you know that He will feed His children and take care of our needs even more so. This shows that God is loving and benevolent toward His children. The fact of the matter is, God invented love. His very nature and essence is love, and He loves you more than you can ever imagine. I believe that one reason why women generally develop a relationship with Jesus more easily than many men do is because, as a male figure, Jesus offers consistent, nonjudgmental love.

Matthew 6:31–32 also reassures us that God is our loving Father who is aware of our needs and takes good care of us: "Don't worry and say, 'What will we eat?' or 'What will we drink?' or 'What will we wear?' The people who don't know God keep trying to get these things, and your Father in heaven knows you need them."

3. There are promises that the heavenly Father has made to you that you need to memorize and quote when you pray. Memorize the following:

"The Father has loved us so much that we are called children of God. And we really are his children" (1 John 3:1).

"If my father and mother leave me, the Lord will take me in" (Psalm 27:10).

"Since you are God's children, God sent the Spirit of his Son into your hearts, and the Spirit cries out, 'Father'" (Galatians 4:6).

"Trust the Lord with all your heart, and don't depend on your own understanding. Remember the Lord in all you do, and he will give you success" (Proverbs 3:5–6).

"I tell you the truth, my Father will give you anything you ask for in my name" (John 16:23).

These are some examples of how we know that the Bible uses the heavenly Father as a model of love. The Bible also uses the earthly father as a model of love. We are talking about the type of love a father should have toward his children.

The Earthly Father Used as a Model of Love

Consider also these Scriptures that explain how God wants earthly fathers to act:

> "The Lord has mercy on those who respect him, as a father has mercy on his children" (Psalm 103:13).
>
> "If your children ask for bread, which of you would give them a stone? Or if your children ask for a fish, would you give them a snake?" (Matthew 7:9–10).
>
> "So hold on through your sufferings, because they are like a father's discipline. God is treating you as children. All children are disciplined by their fathers" (Hebrews 12:7).

These Scriptures are saying that God feels for His children in the same manner that an earthly father feels for his children. Of course, we know that God can love infinitely more than an earthly father, but we see here that the perfect love of God the Father should be modeled in the love of the earthly father toward his children.

Are you loved by an earthly father? If not, your heavenly Father wants to fill the empty space that your earthly father has left. I know of hundreds of women who have successfully done this. You should do this by first of all asking Jesus Christ to forgive you of your sins and then inviting Him to come into your heart. Read the following Scripture, and ask God to help you understand what it means so that you can take these words to heart and claim them for yourself:

> "If you declare with your mouth, 'Jesus is Lord,' and if you believe in your heart that God raised Jesus from the dead, you will be saved. We believe with our hearts, and so we are made right with God. And we declare with our mouths that we believe, and so we are saved" (Romans 10:9–10).

Lastly, ask God to show you a godly woman who has also needed to trust the heavenly Father to fill her need for an earthly father. There should be some ladies like this in your local church, or perhaps at the school that you attend, or maybe even a friend's mom. Through their counsel and guidance you can free your mind from negative thoughts about the concept of fatherhood.

Finally, pray and ask God to provide you with someone who can act as a loving father figure for you. I am a father figure to many young ladies who have no healthy father to guide them. There is someone who will do the same for you. Ask the Lord to help you identify that person.

Think About It

1. What is the first thought that comes to your mind when someone says: "Loving Father."

_____

2. Are you in touch with your true feelings about "fathers" in general and your own biological father? Yes___ No___

3. Have you prayed to God to heal any unhealthy attitudes you may have about your
father? Yes___ No___ Why?
Or why not?

Explain _____

4. Have you forgiven your father for his shortcomings? Yes___ No___
Why? Or why not?

Explain _____

5. Did you realize that forgiving your father is necessary for you to be totally healed from your hurt? Yes___ No___

6. At the beginning of the chapter, the author gives four responses to the pain that some women have regarding absent dads. Which response most accurately
describes you?

_____

7. Find and complete this sentence: "A healthy person understands

_____."

8. Do you know girls who have been hurt by their fathers? Yes___
No___

Are you going to share the information from this chapter with them?
Yes___ No___

34)—Jesus, the Caring Brother

AS A YOUNG WOMAN, the most important thing that you need to know in life is where your father may have failed you. Jesus can help you. The way that you can receive His help is to be sure that you have received His loving gift of salvation. Every human being must give their life to Christ in order to accept this gift that Jesus Christ has made available to us. If you have not already done so, now is the time to find out what salvation in Christ is all about so that you can freely accept this wonderful gift. I want to share some things with you here so that you will have the opportunity to invite Jesus into your life.

The father/daughter relationship is very close to the heart of both fathers and daughters. It is very unfortunate that there are many cases where fathers have caused their daughters pain. In some cases the fathers unknowingly caused the pain, and in other cases the fathers knew that pain would result from their actions. The fact of the matter is that all relationships have the potential at some point to bring you pain.

The world in which we live offers you and me pain on every side. I have found that people respond to the pain of fatherlessness in various ways. Some girls are angry at all men and display that anger in various ways. Other girls have turned their affections toward other females and have chosen not to risk a relationship with a man. Still other women interact with men but are not free to love without fear. I wish that I could offer you a solution to this dilemma that would make all of the pain go away, but there is no quick fix to the problem. What I do recommend for you to do after you have received the free gift of salvation that Jesus has offered you is to develop a relationship with Jesus Christ. God has promised to be a father for anyone who does not have a father. Listen to this Scripture promise:

"God is in his holy Temple. He is a father to orphans, and he defends the widows" (Psalm 68:5).

Having a close relationship with Jesus Christ is the best way to heal any pain your father has caused you. Not only will Jesus heal the pain your father has caused, He is also an expert at healing all other pain in your life. Remember this life offers us pain from many sources. Jesus offers help for all who will call on Him: "Pray to me, and I will answer you. I will tell you important secrets you have never heard before" (Jeremiah 33:3).

Jesus is waiting for you to simply talk to Him like you would talk to a friend. He wants to show you some things that you may not know or understand.

The first thing He wants to show you is how much He loves you.

> "God loved the world so much that he gave his one and only Son so that whoever believes in him may not be lost, but have eternal life" (John 3:16).

God is love and when He thinks of us, His thoughts are loving thoughts. Television programs and movies usually show God's mean side, and they often ignore His loving side. If your dad hurt you, God knows the disappointment you feel about your father, and He is not happy about how you have been treated. "'I say this because I know what I am planning for you,'" says the Lord. "'I have good plans for you, not plans to hurt you. I will give you hope and a good future'" (Jeremiah 29:11).

It is very important that you think about God as a God of love and that you do not blame Him for your earthly father's shortcomings. In time God will heal your heart, and you will see that He is a God of love.

The second thing that God wants you to understand is that nobody is born good in His eyes.

The Word of God explains that every person is born tainted by sin:

> "As the Scriptures say: 'There is no one who always does what is right, not even one'" (Romans 3:10).
>
> "Everyone has sinned and fallen short of God's glorious standard" (Romans 3:23).

We are born without God in our lives. We are born stuck where

Adam and Eve were when God kicked them out of the garden of Eden. Unfortunately, many dads are stuck outside of the garden without God in their lives. It is there (outside the garden) where all pain, lies, abandonment, and dysfunction originate. This is called "sin." It is a state of being where God is not present in our lives.

The third thing that God wants us to understand is that Jesus Christ is the only answer to the sin problem.

This truth is described in Romans 5:19: "One man disobeyed God, and many became sinners. In the same way, one man obeyed God, and many will be made right."

Adam and Eve messed up man's relationship with God. The death, burial, and resurrection of Jesus Christ satisfied God so that through Christ we can have a relationship with God. God loved us so much that He used His own Son to satisfy His anger and the need to judge sin and make a way for man and God to be together again.

Jesus Christ is also called the second Adam because He fixed what the first Adam messed up. In other words, when we are with Jesus, we are in touch with God just like Adam and Eve were before they committed sin.

The fourth thing that God wants us to know and understand is that the ball is now in our court.

It is our turn to make a move. We must individually accept Jesus Christ as our Savior and Lord. We do this by very simply believing that He is God's Son and then asking Him to come into our hearts: "If you declare with your mouth, 'Jesus is Lord,' and if you believe in your heart that God raised Jesus from the dead, you will be saved. We believe with our hearts, and so we are made right with God. And we declare with our mouths that we believe, and so we are saved" (Romans 10:9–10).

The good news is that it is not necessary to feel anything unusual or try to get your life together *before* you ask Him for forgiveness. Once we ask Jesus, He helps us to get our lives together. Once we ask Him to be our Savior, He comes to live in our hearts, and each day He helps us deal with our doubts, disappointments, and yes, even our dads. If you want to ask Jesus to come into your heart, you should pray a prayer something like this:

Dear Jesus, I know that I am a sinner and I need You to help me. Please come into my heart, forgive me of my sins, and be my Lord forever.

Jesus will help you understand and deal with your dad if that is what you need to do. Jesus does not want any young woman to grow up without a dad. But if you are growing up without a dad or with one who is not treating you right, Jesus wants to help you. I want to encourage you to talk to Jesus each day. You can simply share your pain and desires with Him. As you practice doing this, you will sense the peace and satisfaction that He will give you.

Jesus says to us all: "Here I am! I stand at the door and knock. If you hear my voice and open the door, I will come in and eat with you, and you will eat with me" (Revelation 3:20).

Think About It

1. Have you accepted Jesus Christ as your Savior and Lord? Yes___
No___ If yes, have you been baptized? Yes___ No___

2. Do you understand the concept of being born in sin? Yes___ No___

3. Do you believe that Adam and Eve were real people? Yes___ No___

4. What four things does the author say Jesus wants you to know? List
them here:

_____

_____

_____

_____

5. What does Revelation 3:20 promise to anyone who will open the
door?

_____

6. Do you have friends who do not know Jesus Christ? Yes___ No___
Would you be willing to share with them about Jesus? Yes___ No___

7. What Scripture would you use to share Christ with a friend?

_____

_____

8. Are you bold enough to tell your friends that Jesus can be a real dad
for them? Yes___ No___

Name three girls who need to know this:

_____

_____

_____

ISBN-10: 0-8024-4236-6
ISBN-13: 978-0-8024-4236-9

Payton Skky is beautiful and popular and dating Dakari Graham, the most attractive and desirable guy in their Georgia high school. The problem? He wants to have sex with her while she wants to obey God and stay pure until marriage. With pressures coming from all sides, Payton begins to wonder if waiting is really worth it. When he breaks it off with her for a more willing girl, Payton's world crashes down on her. As she struggles to answer these questions and gets to know Tad Taylor, Payton realizes that following God is the real secret to staying pure.

by Stephanie Perry Moore
Find it now at your favorite local or online bookstore.

www.LiftEveryVoiceBooks.com

ISBN-10: 0-8024-4237-4
ISBN-13: 978-0-8024-4237-6

Payton Skky and her girlfriends are in their senior year at their Georgia high school and loving every minute of it. But the rest of Payton's crew has strayed from God and continues to make bad decisions. While chasing after a good time, her friends begin experimenting with alcohol, drugs, and sexual sin. How can Payton help her girls turn toward God and away from those sins? Can she resist her own impulses to try things she knows are against God's will? Come see if Payton discovers how to show her friends that true faith is sober faith.

by Stephanie Perry Moore
Find it now at your favorite local or online bookstore.

www.LiftEveryVoiceBooks.com

The Negro National Anthem

Lift every voice and sing
Till earth and heaven ring,
Ring with the harmonies of Liberty;
Let our rejoicing rise
High as the listening skies,
Let it resound loud as the rolling sea.
Sing a song full of the faith that the dark past has taught us,
Sing a song full of the hope that the present has brought us,
Facing the rising sun of our new day begun
Let us march on till victory is won.

So begins the Black National Anthem by James Weldon Johnson in 1900. Lift Every Voice is the name of the joint imprint of The Institute for Black Family Development and Moody Publishers.

Our vision is to advance the cause of Christ through publishing African-American Christians who educate, edify, and disciple Christians in the church community through quality books written for African Americans.

Since 1988, the Institute for Black Family Development, a 501(c)(3) non-profit Christian organization, has been providing training and technical assistance for churches and Christian organizations. The Institute for Black Family Development's goal is to become a premier trainer in leadership development, management, and strategic planning for pastors, ministers, volunteers, executives, and key staff members of churches and Christian organizations. To learn more about The Institute for Black Family Development write us at:

The Institute for Black Family Development
15151 Faust
Detroit, Michigan 48223

We hope you enjoy this book from Moody Publishers. Our goal is to provide high-quality, thought-provoking books and products that connect truth to your real needs and challenges. For more information on other books and products written and produced from a biblical perspective, go to www.moodypublishers.com or write to:

Moody Publishers/LEV
820 N. LaSalle Boulevard
Chicago, IL 60610
www.moodypublishers.com